THE **MIXER** COOKBOOK

THE **MIXER** COOKBOOK

CLASSIC DELICIOUS RECIPES MADE EFFORTLESSLY

ROSEMARY MOON AND KATIE BISHOP

APPLE

A QUINTET BOOK

Published by Apple Press

Sheridan House

112-116A Western Road

Hove

East Sussex BN3 1DD

ISBN 1 84092 371 7

This book was conceived, designed and produced by

Quintet Publishing Limited

6 Blundell Street

London N7 9BH

Editor: Erin Connell

Photography: Ian Garlick

Food Stylists: Emma Patmore and Jacqueline Bellefontaine

Designer: Janis Utton

Managing Editor: Diana Steedman

Creative Director: Richard Dewing

Publisher: Oliver Salzmann

Manufactured in Singapore by Universal Graphics Pte Ltd

Printed in China by Leefung-Asco Printers Trading Ltd

WARNING

Because of the slight risk of salmonella, raw eggs should not
be served to the very young, the ill or elderly, or to pregnant women.

CONTENTS

INTRODUCTION

Time in the kitchen is at a premium these days – there is a balancing act to perform between working and running the household that results in home cooking too often becoming a casualty of the modern lifestyle.

We all know that home-made food not only tastes best and is nutritionally sound, being free of additives and preservatives, but that people love it. So, a kitchen assistant that can perform the most labour-intensive and repetitive jobs, giving you control of the creative side of cooking without having to worry about the time-consuming grind, is as helpful as an extra pair of hands when it comes to making home baked food for your family and friends.

A table mixer does just that – it takes care of all the hard, time-consuming and heavy jobs that deter so many people from enjoying the pleasures of cooking. Whether you cook for one, two or a crowd, a mixer that will beat, stir, knead and mix will make your life in the kitchen easier and far more pleasurable.

A MULTI-PURPOSE MIXER

Most people can cook when the recipe calls for heating a few ingredients together in a saucepan, or popping a shop-bought pie into the oven. However, the basic techniques of creaming, whisking and kneading often defeat the home cook, or sound too time-consuming even to be attempted on a daily basis. These tasks, however, are the very essence

of a mixer's role, as well as being the foundation of an accomplished cook's skills.

Admittedly, eating habits have changed dramatically over the last decade or so and the pies and cakes of yesteryear are no longer on most day-to-day family menus. **KitchenAid**® stand mixers, and Kenwoods, are however, much more than just mixers for baking. They can be used for mixing any large quantities of food, be it home-made burgers, mashed potatoes, or whisking mayonnaise or salad dressings. Leave your mixer out on the kitchen worktop rather than storing it in a cupboard and you will find more and more uses for it!

PLANETARY ACTION

The best modern mixers employ the most thorough mixing technique ever introduced for domestic food preparation machines – planetary action. This means the beater revolves constantly, while at the same time the hub in which the beater is located moves around the bowl. Thus, every single area of the bowl is reached, ensuring perfect mixing. Just occasionally, a mixture that is very sticky may need to be scraped down the sides of the bowl – this may happen only once or twice during any process

PICK A COLOUR, PICK A STYLE

Gone are the days when kitchen appliances came in only one colour, that being white. Table mixers are now available in a variety of shapes and sizes, and your budget might well dictate choice as much as colour scheme. However, for us, there are only two choices when it comes to mixers – **KitchenAid** or Kenwood.

The **KitchenAid** mixer has a metal construction, with fashionable retro styling. The darling of the modern cook, the company that makes **KitchenAid** mixers is located in St. Joseph, Michigan. The mixers come in a variety of bright, modern colours including scarlet, which is our favourite. The chrome version is the dream of the designer foodie, matching a whole host of desirable, "leave on the worktop" appliances. The advantage of a metal construction is that the mixer is quieter in operation, although neither brand should be thought of as silent! It is also more robust but, of course, these features carry a price tag, so you may need to consider what is right for you. The **KitchenAid** mixer has a range of optional attachments which cover the basic, time-consuming tasks that are tackled in the kitchen.

Kenwood offers The Chef and The Major, the latter being a large capacity machine suitable for domestic or light commercial usage. Both mix, whisk and knead and have a wide range of attachments to take on many kitchen tasks, including a liquidiser for blending, making soups and drinks and breadcrumbs. The original Kenwood Chef was all metal (apart from the bowl, which was glass). Now usually styled in white, with either a white or stainless steel bowl, Kenwoods are also available in colours, the choices having changed considerably over the years to match prevailing kitchen fashions. For fifty years or more, these machines have been made in the United Kingdom and are now gracing the kitchens of busy cooks worldwide.

THE RIGHT TOOL FOR THE RIGHT JOB

This has always been, and still remains, a cooking teacher's favourite catch-phrase! And it's quite right, too – you can't coax air into a mixture for perfectly light pastry or fluffy meringues and mousses, let alone knead bread dough for a perfect rise, with a blade in a food processor that has really been designed for chopping. Table mixers have the following three basic tools, which are perfect for basic mixing jobs:

- The flat beater: the workhorse beater, to be used for cutting in butter or margarine, creaming, stirring meat and vegetable mixtures, and all general mixing and beating.
- The wire whip or whisk: for all whisking jobs, including egg whites, double cream, sponge cakes, and so on. Also great for beating the lumps out of sauces and custards!
- The dough hook: for kneading yeast mixtures into perfectly smooth, silky and tensile doughs.

TO ATTACH THE BEATERS

With the mixer switched off, simply raise the head of your mixer and affix the required beater onto the mixer shaft, turning it slightly to lock into position. Unlock and remove the beaters in the same way.

The beaters are usually suitable for cleaning in a dishwasher, although we prefer to wash the metal beaters by hand to maintain their finish. It's great to be able to put the white coated blades of the **KitchenAid** mixer into the dishwasher, and they do wash up very well, but remember to rinse them first, especially after making bread dough and if you are not going to run the dishwasher immediately..

 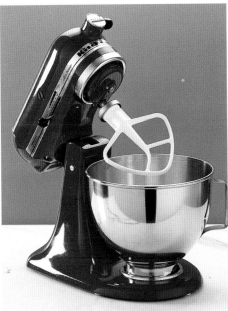 

Left Wire whip   **Middle** Flat beater   **Right** Dough hook

GETTING READY TO MIX

When you remove your mixer from the box, it should be perfectly adjusted and ready for use. A basic rule of thumb is that you should be able to just fit a sheet of paper between the beaters and the bottom of the bowl; use the flat beater to check. If adjustments should be necessary, it is simply done with the turn of a screw. Please refer to your mixer instruction book for details.

BASIC MIXING TIPS

As much common sense and a way to keep the kitchen free from flying flour as anything else!

- Always start mixing at a slow speed.
- Gradually add extra ingredients.
- Add ingredients down the side of the bowl or down the chute of the pouring shield to avoid excessive splashing while the mixer is running.
- Fold in fruit, flavourings and flour at the end of recipes

using a very low speed to avoid knocking out the air.

- Some yeasted doughs that require blending or rubbing the butter or margarine into the flour at the beginning of mixing are best started with the flat beater. However, it is important to change to the dough hook to mix in the liquid and to knead the dough.
- Whisking should always be started on a slow speed and then gradually increased until the mixture is frothy, and then increased further to a faster whisking speed. Whisking too quickly will incorporate less air, leading to a closer-textured and heavier final result.
- Whisk egg whites at room temperature for the best possible results.
- Keep an eye on cream when whipping it. It can suddenly thicken, especially if you are whisking a large quantity. Adding a little milk and whisking again can sometimes rescue cream that has been whipped too much.
- We like to have two bowls for our mixers, which is

Left Rotary Slicer and Shredder **Middle** Food Grinder **Right** Pasta Maker

especially useful if you are making a mixture with egg whites added at the end, making bread and doing other cooking at the same time, or cooking for a party and making lots of different dishes.

ADDING ATTACHMENTS TO YOUR MIXER

We have selected our favourite table mixer attachments for this book, but you should check which of these are available for your mixer and, of course, check out other attachments designed for your machine.

ROTARY SLICER AND SHREDDER

One of the most useful attachments – and the one that you will see featured most frequently in our recipes. It is great for making salads and preparing bulk quantities of vegetables. There are two basic types of attachment, one

with drums and one with plates, the latter being "high speed", although both yield quicker results than a sharp knife even deftly wielded. Check out which type of attachment is available for your mixer.

We sometimes make potato casseroles for a quick dinner dish. Peel about 750 g of potatoes and process them through the slicer with two or three onions. Layer them in a buttered baking dish with lots of salt and pepper and about 300 g of marinated sardines or anchovies spread out between the layers and a sprinkle of sugar. Pour 500 ml/two cups of milk over the potatoes, drizzle the top layer with olive oil and bake at 190°C/Gas Mark 5 for an hour, until browned and the potatoes are tender. Serve with fresh green vegetables, or a green or a tomato salad. Coleslaw is also a favourite of ours and it's so easy with this attachment. Slice half a cabbage into the mixer bowl, then grate in two carrots and one small onion using the

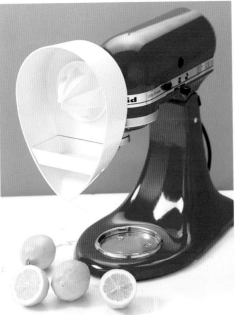

Left Sausage Maker **Middle** Citrus Juicer **Right** Can Opener

coarse drum. Add lots of salt and pepper and mayonnaise, then mix with the flat beater to combine.

FOOD GRINDER

This is another very useful attachment, good for making pâtés and essential if you wish to make your own sausages. It is also the best way of making home-made burgers, pasta sauces and other dishes made with ground meat, because you can be utterly confident that you are using the best-quality ground meat or poultry since you are mincing it yourself. The attachment comes with two plates to offer a coarse or a fine mince. The best tips we can offer on usage are:

- Always be sure that the grinder shaft is properly located in the mixer power outlet, or the food will not be fed through the attachment.
- The knife goes onto the shaft before the grinding plate and then the locking nut is used to hold the attachment

together. Do not tighten it too much.

- Cut away as much gristle and sinew from the meat as possible (including "tubey" bits) as these tend to become tangled around the knife.
- Always cut meat into strips, not chunks, to feed through the grinder and always use the stomper that has been provided to guide the meat through.

We sometimes use the grinder for preparing marmalade. It will not give quite as clear a result as cutting the peel by hand, but it does save a huge amount of time. Squeeze the juice from the fruit, pull out the membrane and pith and tie it in a muslin bag as directed by your favourite recipe. Mince the peel using the coarse plate. Cooking time will also be shortened, as the peel will be in smaller and softer pieces than when cut by hand. We generally just boil the peel in the recommended amount of water until it has reduced as required — no additional simmering time appears necessary. Add the sugar and proceed as usual.

PASTA MAKER

We love making our own pasta, so a pasta attachment is pretty important to us both. Some mixers have a pasta extruder, which will give macaroni-type shapes, but that requires a very dry dough being dropped into it in tiny pieces. Our favourite, though more limited in the shapes it can produce, is a roller-type attachment, which makes flat lasagne sheets as well as tagliatelle and linguine. After mixing the dough, it is passed repeatedly through the rollers until the sheets are smooth and of the required thickness, at which point cutting rollers can be fitted and the pasta cut into lengths.

- Always clear and lightly flour a large surface before making pasta so you have plenty of room to lay the lengths out without damaging them.
- Don't allow the dough to dry out at any stage in the process. If you have to leave the dough, always cover it with clingfilm or a teatowel.
- Don't be afraid to roll the dough out over and over again. The more thorough you are during this part of the process, the better the end result will be. Under-worked dough will produce tough, chewy pasta.
- Depending on the quantity of dough, it is generally easier to divide it into manageable "lumps" (usually four) before feeding it through the rollers. This avoids getting tied up in long lengths of pasta and makes it far easier to handle, especially when using the cutting rollers.

If you make your own pasta, and you certainly will with this attachment, it is a good idea to try to match the consistency of the sauce to be served with the shape of the pasta. Chunky sauces are best cooked with lasagnes, while smooth sauces are great with fine pastas, and those sauces with prawns and small chunks are good with tagliatelle. Of course, these rules are not set in stone, but they do make eating pasta without getting splattered with sauce just a little bit easier!

SAUSAGE MAKER

Sausages are one of the largest and fastest-growing sectors of the fresh meat market. Quick to cook and available in many designer flavours, they fit in well with hectic lifestyles and adventurous palettes. The sausage maker attachment is great fun and, again, it enables you to ensure that your family is eating the highest-quality meat.

A certain amount of skill is required to produce a professional-looking sausage, especially if you are going to twist them into links as they come through the attachment! You will need casing, which should be natural skins that your butcher can supply. (If you are unable to obtain these from your butcher, see page 158 for details of international distributors.) They have to be soaked and then threaded onto the attachment without splitting. Keep the skins in water until needed and then catch a little water in one end to open it up for threading onto the attachment.

Mince your meat and then mix it with seasonings and a small amount of breadcrumbs to bind it together when mixed in the bowl with the flat beater. Try mincing a boned shoulder of lamb with a couple of shallots and one or two cloves of garlic, and then adding a small handful of stoned dates or dried apricots and mince them too, before passing some bread through the grinder to make breadcrumbs. Spice with mint, cumin, coriander and a little crushed chilli ground together. Remove the grinder screen and blade and fit the sausage filler, but ensure that the grinder drive shaft is still secure in the mixer power outlet. (Once you have meat all over your hands you won't want to be dismantling the attachment to see why the meat isn't coming through into the skins.) Feed the meat through slowly and evenly, holding the skins over the nozzle until they are sufficiently filled. Twist the skins every so often to form sausage links. We suggest that you leave the sausages for an hour or two before you cook them, which helps the meat to hold all its moisture.

CITRUS JUICER

For large quantities of juicing, this is a real time saver. Use it when preparing Grapefruit Sorbet (page 104), Seriously Lemony Lemon Bars (page 123) or any other recipe containing citrus. And of course, it's really wonderful for making marmalade too, when used in conjunction with the grinder. Home-made lemonade is a real treat in the summer, especially after a hard game of tennis or even some serious relaxing!

Pare the rinds of six large, unwaxed lemons with a potato peeler, place in a large jug with 200 g of caster sugar and add 2 litres/8 cups of boiling water. Leave for one hour. Squeeze the juice from the lemons using the Citrus Juicer and add it to the jug, then strain the mixture and chill, or serve over ice.

CAN OPENER

Keep your mixer out on the work surface with the can opener in place and it will always be there, ready for action. This heavy-duty opener can tackle tiny cans of tomato purée all the way up to extra-large cans of vegetables and coffee. Always keep the blades wiped clean

 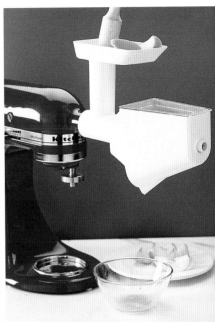

Left Grain Mill **Right** Fruit and Vegetable Strainer

and remove any paper and torn labels that collect and gather around the blades.

OTHER ATTACHMENTS

A strainer and a wheat or grain mill are among the other attachments available for table mixers. The latter is useful for producing more unusual flours, either from beans or grains, especially for those who don't have access to health-food stores.

Some attachments do the job of separate, stand-alone appliances and it is up to you to decide which will get used the most – an attachment for your mixer to be fitted before use, or a worktop appliance. Always be sure that working parts of attachments and other appliances are suitable for cleaning in the dishwasher.

BLUEPRINTS
FOR SUCCESS

Using your mixer is really very straightforward. Just select the

appropriate beater and off you go. However, we have selected the

tasks that our mixers are used for most frequently and here are our

hints and tips for culinary success.

If you have been used to creaming cakes with a wooden spoon and rubbing fat into flour for pastry with your fingers, you will soon realise the meaning of the term 'labour-saving' appliance, as your mixer really does do all the hard work for you.

To get the very best results from your machine, however, it is important to know a little about the techniques and tasks that are being performed on your behalf – the basic science that supports cooking. Why should you use plain flour with no raising agent for whisked sponges when you need flour and a raising agent for creamed mixtures? And why do we say self-raising flour plus additional raising agent when we make an all-in-one cake?

In this section we cover the culinary skills that you will tackle with your mixer, and we have explained the rules and basic theory behind each method. Of course, rules in cooking are there to be broken and many wonderful dishes are born through pushing the boundaries of flavour and texture combinations, but even the most exciting dishes are based on classical techniques. Exact proportions

are critical for baking and puddings, as well as for pastries and mayonnaise, and these are the foundations of most of the dishes in this book.

We have also included some hints and tips as to how each mixture should be made – the best ingredients to use, the preferred method or order of mixing, any possible pitfalls to look out for and, occasionally, a rescue plan should anything go wrong! (Which it does for us all.)

Occasionally we say to use a beater that you might feel is an odd choice, but, rest assured, there is good reason for this! So, when we say mix the Lemonade Scones (page 131) with the dough hook on the slowest possible speed, we do mean the dough hook – although a classic scone would be mixed with the flat beater.

These blueprints will ensure repeated culinary triumphs for you and your mixer. Read them all now, or flick back and pick out the appropriate section before tackling a new recipe. Either way, it's all very useful information – and a vital ingredient for success.

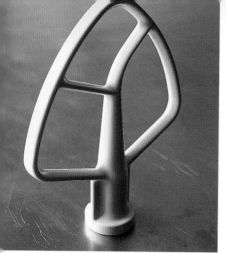

SCONE DOUGH

A scone is a quick sweet or savoury "bread" made without yeast. It is soft and light on the inside and golden and crusty on the outside, served baked in a round or wedge-shape. Scones can be eaten warm or cold.

- Made from any variety of flours, either self-raising or plain and a raising agent.
- Scones rise due to the chemical action of the raising agent.
- Butter or margarine can be used, although butter has a far superior flavour.
- Contains a small proportion of butter or margarine to flour.
- Fresh milk, buttermilk or yoghurt is used to bind the mixture and to encourage the chemical raising action.
- The texture should be light and fairly open.
- Scones are best eaten on day they are made.

BASIC METHOD

- Sieve flour, raising agent and salt into mixer bowl.
- Add butter or margarine.
- Use the flat beater or dough hook at slow to medium speed to combine until the mixture resembles breadcrumbs.
- Add nearly all the liquid, all at once.
- Mix again at slow to moderate speed until dough is smooth, springy and elastic. Add remaining extra liquid if required.
- Roll out on a lightly floured surface to thickness of about 2 cm.
- Cut into rounds or wedges.
- Put onto greased and floured baking tray.
- Brush with milk or beaten egg.
- Bake in preheated hot oven for about 10 to 15 minutes.

VARIATIONS

- Use wholemeal flour, or half wholemeal and half plain flour.
- Add grated cheese or dried fruits.

BASIC HINTS FOR SUCCESS

- Handle the dough lightly.
- Keep the ingredients cool.
- Work quickly.
- Always preheat the oven.
- Always sieve the flour before using, whether self-raising or plain.
- Always sieve the raising agent, if using, with the flour so it is evenly distributed.
- Don't over-work the dough, as this will result in heavy and badly risen scones.
- Don't over-grease the baking tray, as this will encourage the scones to spread and lose their shape.

SHORTCRUST PASTRY

Shortcrust pastry is the most commonly used pastry as it is so versatile. It is also the easiest to make. Your mixer makes pastry quickly with a minimum amount of handling. It is made by the rubbing in, or blending, method.

- Pastry of any description works because of accurately proportioned butter or margarine, flour and liquid.
- Standard shortcrust pastry has a ratio of half butter or margarine to flour.
- Increasing the butter or margarine, or whatever type of fat you use, will make the pastry even shorter.
- Butter, margarine, lard or solid vegetable shortening can be used depending upon the desired flavour and texture.
- Butter alone produces a rich pastry.
- Butter and vegetable shortening makes a rich, light pastry.
- Adding egg yolk will make the pastry shorter, as the fat content is increased.

BASIC METHOD

- Sieve the four and salt into the mixer bowl.
- Add the fat.
- Use the flat beater at slow to moderate speed until the mixture resembles breadcrumbs.
- Add ice-cold water a spoonful at a time until the mixture begins to come together.
- Use your hands to gather the mixture into a ball.
- Cover in clingfilm and refrigerate for 30 minutes.

TO ROLL OUT

- Lightly flour a roomy surface.
- Use short, sharp movements away from you and work as quickly as possible, turning the pastry frequently to ensure that it does not stick to the surface.
- If rolling for a specific tin, allow for the base and sides of the tin, with a little extra to spare.

- The higher the butter or margarine content, the harder the pastry will be to roll out. Very short sweet pastry can be pressed into the tin with no adverse effect on the final result.
- Don't stretch your pastry or it will shrink during cooking. Also ensure that the pastry is pushed into the corners of the pan with your finger to keep a good shape.

TO COOK

- To bake pastry blind: line the uncooked pastry case with foil or greaseproof paper and fill with pie weights, dried beans or rice, and bake. Cool before filling.

BASIC HINTS FOR SUCCESS

- Always work quickly and with cold ingredients, utensils and hands, and handle as little as possible.
- Do not over-mix, as this will toughen the pastry.
- Too much liquid will also toughen the pastry.

SPONGE OR SANDWICH CAKES

These cakes are usually made by the creaming or whisking methods.

CREAMED SPONGE

- Creaming fat and sugar together incorporates air into the mixture. Insufficient creaming will result in a dense, heavy and/or coarse cake.
- Eggs are then added, a little at a time, and beaten well between each addition. Flour is folded in last, lightly at a slow speed, so as not to knock out all the air that has already been incorporated.
- The final mixture should be light and creamy.

BASIC METHOD

- Using the flat beater at moderate speed, "cream" the butter or margarine and sugar together until light, fluffy and pale in colour. Use caster sugar or light brown sugar as their smaller crystals will incorporate into the butter or margarine better than other varieties with larger granules.
- Add beaten eggs gradually, combining fully after each addition.
- Add any liquid to the mixture and combine.
- Sieve the flour, salt, baking powder (if using) and any additional ingredients into the mixer bowl in two or three stages at a slow speed. The final mixture is usually a soft, dropping consistency and flicks easily off a spoon.
- Spoon into the prepared tin(s) and make a dip in the centre to prevent the mixture from forming a peak during baking. This is particularly relevant if the mixture contains a high proportion of fruit.
- Bake in oven preheated to a moderate to high heat.
- Usually position the tin(s) on the middle shelf.

BASIC HINTS FOR SUCCESS

- Measure and weigh ingredients as accurately as possible – correct proportions are essential.
- We strongly believe that where possible, butter should be used for making cakes. The flavour is undoubtedly superior.
- Use butter at room temperature or softened slightly.
- Use eggs at room temperature to prevent curdling. A curdled mixture will not hold as much air.
- If curdling occurs, add a tablespoon of flour and incorporate gently.
- Always sieve flour and raising agent.
- Always grease baking tins and base-line with baking parchment unless otherwise stated.
- Always preheat the oven. Never open the door during cooking – the cake may sink.
- To test if cakes are cooked, press lightly – the mixture should be firm and spring back when touched.

VICTORIA SANDWICH

This classic cake is usually made using the creaming method above and is cooked in two tins of equal size. When cooked and cooled, the cakes are sandwiched together with jam and topped with a sprinkling of sugar.

Alternatively, fill with fruit, buttercream, whipped cream, fruit curd, sweetened cream cheese or unsweetened yoghurt (see page 117).

ALL-IN-ONE METHOD

You can make an excellent sponge cake in very little time by beating all the ingredients together at once. This is particularly effective when using a mixer, as thorough beating is essential.

For success, however, the following guidelines apply:
• The butter or margarine must be soft to ensure that it incorporates easily.
• An extra raising agent is required, as not engaging in an initial creaming process results in less air being incorporated into the mixture

BASIC METHOD

• Put all ingredients into the mixer bowl and combine using the flat beater at slow to medium speed. Use softened butter or margarine.
• Spoon mixture into prepared tin(s).
• Bake in a preheated oven.

WHISKED SPONGE CAKE

Your mixer is perfect for this method, as very thorough whisking makes a perfect cake. The sponge is made by whisking eggs and sugar together to incorporate air and then adding flour to give it structure.

- Plain flour is always used for whisked sponges, as self-raising flour can cause the cake to rise too much and then collapse.
- No raising agent is added.
- The texture is a light, open structure with a crisp surface.
- Due to rapid drying out, whisked sponges are always best eaten on the day they are baked.

BASIC METHOD

- Use the wire whip to whisk the eggs lightly, then add the sugar and whisk at full speed for about 10 minutes or until the mixture leaves a trail when the wire whip is removed.
- The mixture will be pale in colour and will have greatly increased in volume.
- Gradually fold in the sieved flour with a metal spoon.
- Pour into a prepared tin.
- Bake in a preheated oven.

BASIC HINTS FOR SUCCESS

- Always use very fresh eggs at room temperature for better whisking.
- Use caster sugar for a smoother, more even texture.
- Warm the bowl slightly before beginning the recipe.
- Use all ingredients at room temperature or slightly warmed.
- Always fold flour into the mixture gently with a metal spoon to avoid knocking out any air.
- Always preheat the oven.
- Usually position the tin(s) on a middle shelf.
- To test if the cake is cooked, press lightly and your finger should leave no impression in the cake.
- Remove from the tin and cool, right side up, on a wire rack to avoid getting patterns on the cake. Ensure that the cake does not cool in a draught, as a sudden change in temperature usually makes the cake shrivel.

MERINGUE

Made from egg whites (see note, page 4) and sugar, meringue can be dried out in the oven very slowly until crisp, or used as a soft topping when baked very quickly at a high temperature.

- The most common method of making a meringue is by adding dry sugar to whisked egg whites.
- Meringue may be piped, spread or spooned into shapes.

BASIC METHOD

- Place egg whites in a scrupulously clean mixer bowl.
- Whisk the whites until very stiff and dry, starting slowly and getting faster.
- Add sugar a third at a time, whisking thoroughly between each addition. Alternatively, with the mixer and wire whip running at moderate speed, add the sugar a teaspoonful at a time, being careful not to over-whisk.
- Spoon over a pudding, into tins or pipe into required shapes.
- Cook very briefly in a very hot oven to serve as a topping.
- For dry meringue shells, cook at a very low temperature for a much longer period of time.

BASIC HINTS FOR SUCCESS

- Use eggs that are two to three days old, by which time the white will have lost some water through evaporation. This makes the whites more gelatinous and therefore easier to whip. The mixture is also easier to use in this condition.
- Traditionalists separate their eggs and let the whites stand for 24 hours before using for the same reasons, although this is far from essential and rarely done in domestic kitchens today.
- Always use a spotlessly clean wire whip and bowl, as any trace of fat or dirt will prevent the white from whisking satisfactorily.
- Always whisk in a cool environment.
- Use caster sugar, as this is less damaging to the unstable proteins in the egg whites.
- Always add the sugar gradually and whisk it in thoroughly between each addition.
- Use the raw meringue immediately to prevent warm air from affecting the structure of the protein. If allowed to stand, the meringue will become watery and lose its shape.
- Never hurry drying meringue or you will produce soft, leathery results.
- Store dried meringues in airtight containers. They will keep for several weeks.

MAYONNAISE

Mayonnaise is a thick and creamy "emulsified" sauce where oil (traditionally olive) is dispersed and suspended in vinegar with the assistance of an emulsifying agent – egg yolk (see note, page 4). Mayonnaise is usually flavoured with mustard, vinegar, lemon juice, salt and pepper. It can be made effortlessly with the wire whip on your mixer.

BASIC METHOD

- Put egg yolks, mustard, salt and pepper into the mixer bowl.
- Using the wire whip, combine at medium speed.
- With the mixer set at fast speed, add the oil very gradually, ensuring it is fully combined between each addition.
- The mixture will gradually thicken, increase in volume and become creamy in consistency. The colour will become whiter as beating continues.
- Add vinegar, lemon juice and seasoning to taste.
- Refrigerate for up to two weeks before serving.
- If the mixture curdles, continue whisking and add a little vinegar or lemon juice. If this doesn't fix the problem, whisk more egg yolk(s) separately and gradually whisk the curdled mixture into it.

BASIC HINTS FOR SUCCESS

- Always use ingredients at room temperature.
- Always use the best-quality oil you can afford.
- Never rush the addition of oil or the mixture will curdle immediately.
- Some people find an all olive oil mayonnaise too rich and strong in flavour, so experiment to find the right taste for you. Try light olive oil, or a mix of olive and other oils.

MOUSSE

A mousse is a light, whipped, sweet or savoury mixture made easily with your mixer.

- It is usually made with a base of smooth fruit or vegetable purée.
- Stiffly whisked egg whites (see note, page 4) are often incorporated to open the texture of the mixture.
- Egg yolk can be added to create a richer mousse.
- Mousses are usually "set" with gelatin, cream, béchamel sauce or sometimes mayonnaise.
- Generous seasoning is essential for savoury dishes.
- Use quality ingredients to ensure a good flavour.

BASIC METHOD

- Use a clean wire whip to whip cream and other basic ingredients.
- Add dissolved gelatin and mix thoroughly; add a little of the whisked mixture to the dissolved gelatin and then whisk that into the mixture.
- Season very generously for savoury dishes.
- Chill lightly. When starting to set, whisk egg whites and then fold them into the mixture.
- Pour into prepared moulds and chill until set; aspic may be used as a base in the mould for savoury mousse.
- Dip the moulds in warm water to loosen and turn out.

BASIC HINTS FOR SUCCESS

- When dissolving gelatin, add it to hot water and stir. DO NOT boil gelatin.
- Use the correct ratio of gelatin to liquid.
- Always season mousse thoroughly, as chilling will inhibit most flavours.

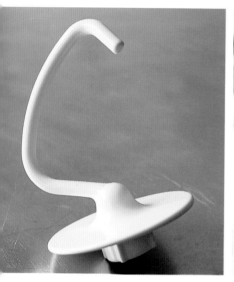

BREAD

Bread is a baked dough usually risen by yeast. Using the dough hook on your mixer takes all the hard work out of bread making and saves on time, too.

- Most breads are made by combining flour with yeast and liquid.
- The dough is kneaded, left to rise, shaped, left to rise again and baked.

- **The Flour** – the bulk of most bread dough. Plain flour, or bread flour, is preferable.
- All flour contains gluten, an elastic protein that is essential to hold the carbon dioxide that is given off by yeast. During and after baking, gluten hardens around the bubbles of carbon dioxide, thus giving the bread its risen shape.
- Kneading is required to stretch and strengthen the gluten, which makes it more elastic.
- The gluten becomes tough and leathery when baked if the dough is insufficiently kneaded.

- **The Yeast** – a natural raising agent which gives off carbon dioxide as it grows.
- In order to grow, yeast must have moisture, warmth, food and time.
- Sugar is essential if using conventional dried yeast, as it "feeds" it. Fresh yeast will usually feed on the natural sugars in the flour. Honey can also be used.
- Salt is essential for flavour, but more importantly, it strengthens the gluten in the flour. This prevents the dough from rising too quickly.
- Butter, margarine or oil is an important addition, as it adds moisture to the dough and improves keeping quality. It is not, however, essential.
- Milk, water, or a combination of the two, may be used in the mixture. The amount varies according to the type of flour used.
- The temperature of the liquid should be just above body temperature. Too low a temperature won't activate the yeast and too high a temperature will kill it.
- Fresh yeast – Usually found in a block, fresh yeast is similar in appearance to putty. It is fairly crumbly and can

be broken easily. If it is fresh enough, the yeast should have a fruity aroma. Stale yeast develops an unpleasant odour that will taint the bread. Fresh yeast is creamed with warm liquid to activate it.

- Dried yeast – Available in containers or individual packets, it is granular and light brown or beige in colour. It must be rehydrated with warm liquid and activated with a small amount of sugar. It also needs about 15 minutes to "wake up" before use!
- Easy-blend dried yeast – Available in packets, this granular yeast is simply added directly to the flour together with remaining ingredients. Using easy blend dry yeast usually means that the bread will only require one proving. Always read the manufacturers' label.

BASIC METHOD

- Add the flour and salt into the mixer bowl.
- Cream the yeast with a little warm liquid. Alternatively, if using conventional dried yeast, add the packet and sugar to the warm liquid. The liquid should be just warm to the touch. (If using easy blend dry yeast, add the packet to the flour, followed by the remaining ingredients.)
- Add to the flour and using the dough hook at slow to medium speed, combine the ingredients thoroughly.
- Knead for a few minutes until the dough is smooth and elastic and leaves the sides of the bowl.
- If using easy blend dry yeast, shape as desired and leave to rise, covered, in chosen tin or on a baking tray for 30 to 40 minutes.
- For other yeasts, leave the dough in the mixer bowl, cover and set aside in a warm place until the dough has doubled in size. Then, using the dough hook, knead again and shape. Leave in a warm place until doubled in size once more.

- Bake in a hot oven.
- To test for doneness, tap the bottom of the bread. It should sound hollow.

BASIC HINTS FOR SUCCESS

- Always use "healthy" yeast; check use-by date and ensure that the yeast smells and looks right before you begin.
- Always add salt for flavour, even if making sweet bread.
- Make sure the liquid to be added is at the correct temperature – it should be lukewarm, not hot.
- Always knead thoroughly to ensure even distribution of yeast and therefore gas.
- Unless using easy blend dry yeast, never rush the kneading or proving process.
- Let bread rise in warm conditions – too hot an environment will cause the dough to be heavy, too cool and nothing will happen.
- Always cook in a preheated hot oven.

LIGHT
LUNCHES

Easy dishes for meals in a rush, these are favourite recipes for times when one course is just what you want, whether it's a substantial snack or a light main dish. Some of the recipes, such as our Creamy Corn Cornbread (page 32), require some preparation and a serious amount of cooking time, but then the finished dish is there as a substantial snack whenever you like.

GAZPACHO

SERVES 4 TO 6

PREPARATION TIME: 15 minutes

CHILLING TIME: at least 1 hour,
 preferably overnight

**750 g ripe tomatoes, cores
 removed**

1 red pepper, deseeded

1 green pepper, deseeded

1 red onion, peeled

½ cucumber, deseeded

2 garlic cloves, finely chopped

1 Tbsp finely chopped parsley

**1 Tbsp finely chopped fresh
 basil leaves**

1½ Tbsp red wine vinegar

125 ml/½ cup passata

80 ml/⅓ cup water

3 drops Tabasco

4 Tbsp olive oil

**Salt and freshly ground black
 pepper to taste**

*Gazpacho is a classic summer soup from Spain and is easy to make with
your mixer. This recipe does not use breadcrumbs – just fresh
Mediterranean vegetables.*

1 Coarsely grate the vegetables into the mixer bowl using the Rotary Slicer and
Shredder.

2 Add all the other ingredients and mix thoroughly with the flat beater,
seasoning well with salt and pepper. Refrigerate for 12 hours if possible, to
allow the flavours to mellow and blend (see Cook's Tip).

3 Serve this soup with cubes of frozen olive oil, some fresh basil leaves and our
Cheese Sablé biscuits (see below).

COOK'S TIP: The gazpacho is best eaten chilled and when fresh, but it will
keep well for up to three days in the refrigerator.

CHEESE SABLES

MAKES ABOUT 40

PREPARATION TIME: 15 minutes

COOKING TIME: 10 minutes

100 g Cheddar cheese

100 g butter

125 g plain flour

Pinch of salt

Pinch of dry mustard

*These lightest and richest of cheese biscuits will disappear as quickly as
you can make them! Great by themselves, or with Gazpacho.*

1 Preheat the oven to 200°C/Gas Mark 6 and lightly butter two baking trays.

2 Grate the cheese into the mixing bowl. Add the butter, and cream together
with the flat beater until light and soft. Add the flour, salt, and mustard and mix
slowly until the mixture forms a stiff dough. Add just a little extra flour if
necessary.

3 Roll the dough out on a lightly floured surface to 5-mm thickness and cut into
rounds approximately 4 cm across. Arrange on the baking trays and prick lightly
with a fork. Continue re-rolling the dough until it is all used up.

4 Bake for 10 minutes until lightly golden, then cool on a wire tray before
serving.

SALMON AND CREAM CHEESE BAGEL PUFFS

Choux pastry, which is usually eaten filled with cream and topped with chocolate, is easy to make with your mixer. The pastry makes a great, light alternative to bagels for our favourite filling of smoked salmon and cream cheese – a perfect TV snack.

....

1 Preheat the oven to 220°C/Gas Mark 7 and lightly butter a baking tray. Sieve the flour onto kitchen paper and add the salt.

2 Melt the butter in the water in a saucepan over a low heat, then bring to a rapid boil. Add the flour and beat quickly with a wooden spoon until mixed, then pour into the mixer bowl and beat on a medium speed for one minute, or until the mixture leaves the sides of the bowl cleanly. Allow to cool for a few minutes.

3 Gradually add the beaten egg, mixing slowly at first, and then a little faster. The mixture should hold its shape, so only add as much of the egg as is necessary. Scoop the pastry out in six large spoonfuls and place on the baking tray, flattening the piles slightly into round, bagel-like shapes. Bake in the preheated oven for 25 to 30 minutes until browned and crisp.

4 Reduce the heat to 190°C/Gas Mark 5. Carefully slit the puffs with a knife to allow the steam to escape and then bake for another 10 to 15 minutes until thoroughly dry and crisp. Cool on a wire rack.

5 To serve, split each puff with a knife and fill with cream cheese, smoked salmon, and gherkins or capers. Add the mock caviar and some salad leaves if you wish, then top with the remaining pastry and garnish with chives.

....

COOK'S TIP: Bread flour makes the crispest choux pastry. It is essential to add the flour to the water and butter when it is boiling to get the correct consistency in the pastry; sieving the flour onto greaseproof paper so that you can pour it straight into the saucepan is the easiest way to do this.

MAKES 6 PUFFS
PREPARATION TIME: 15 minutes
COOKING TIME: 45 minutes

100 g bread flour
Pinch of salt
**50 g butter, cut into small
   pieces**
150 ml/⅔ cup water
2 eggs, beaten

FILLING
200 g cream cheese
6 large slices smoked salmon
Sliced gherkins and capers
**Fish roe, such as black herring
   or lumpfish (optional)**

**Lettuce, baby spinach leaves,
   or rocket and chives to
   garnish (optional)**

CREAMY CORN CORNBREAD

MAKES 1 LARGE LOAF
PREPARATION TIME: 40 minutes
COOKING TIME: 45 minutes

3 eggs, separated
420-g can creamed sweet
   corn
140 ml/⅔ cup double cream
100 g butter, melted
50 g Gruyère cheese, finely
   grated
100 g yellow cornmeal or
   instant polenta
125 g self-raising flour
1 tsp baking powder
1 tsp caster sugar
1 Tbsp dried chilli flakes
   (optional)
½ tsp salt

This loaf is almost a meal in itself – try it spread with cream cheese! It can also be sliced and served with cold meats or fish and salad. It's addictive!

1 Preheat the oven to 190°C/Gas Mark 5 and oil a 23-cm round cake tin with corn oil.

2 Beat the egg yolks with the corn, double cream, melted butter and cheese on a low speed to combine, using the flat beater. Add all the dry ingredients and beat for a minute or so until completely blended. Transfer to another bowl and wash the mixer bowl.

3 Whisk the egg whites until stiff with the wire whip, starting slowly and gradually increasing to a medium-high speed. Fold the egg whites evenly into the corn mixture, then pour into the prepared cake tin.

4 Bake for 45 minutes until lightly browned and set. Loosen the cornbread from the sides of the tin and turn out carefully onto a wire rack. Cool slightly before slicing and serving.

COOK'S TIP: The cornbread will puff up slightly like a soufflé during baking and then fall back a little – don't worry, this is normal!

LINGUINE WITH CHILLI, CRAB AND VERMOUTH

**SERVES 4 AS A LIGHT MAIN
    COURSE OR STARTER**
**PREPARATION TIME: about 25
    minutes**
COOKING TIME: 5 TO 10 MINUTES

PASTA DOUGH:
250 g plain flour
2 eggs
1 egg yolk

FOR THE SAUCE:
50 g butter
4 Tbsp olive oil
**2 large cloves garlic, finely
    chopped**
**1 small red chilli, finely
    chopped**
**12 cherry tomatoes,
    quartered**
170-g can white crab meat
2 Tbsp vermouth
**3 Tbsp flat-leaf parsley, finely
    chopped**
**Salt and freshly ground black
    pepper to taste**

Lemon wedges to serve

Pasta is easy and quick to make with a table mixer. Make it in advance, and when you're ready to eat, it takes less than two minutes to cook. Some people insist on using pasta flour, salt and olive oil in their dough, but this recipe wins for us every time. We find ordinary flour ideal (and far less expensive!); salt can sometimes toughen the egg, making the pasta leathery; and the addition of olive oil seems unnecessary.

....

1 Make the pasta. Combine the flour and eggs in the mixer bowl using the dough hook, initially at slow speed and gradually increasing to medium. Mix for about three minutes, then, if necessary, bring the dough together with your hands.

2 Cut the dough into four pieces and, using your pasta roller attachment on the lowest setting, run each piece of dough through the machine. Fold up the rolled dough and run it through again. Repeat this process about 10 to 15 times until the dough becomes shiny and almost leathery to the touch. Then, put the machine up a notch and feed the dough through again, continuing this process until you reach setting 5. Change the attachment to the linguine (fine) drum and feed each piece of dough through. Lightly toss flour through the pasta and reserve, well covered, in a cool place.

3 Bring a large pan of salted water to the boil. Meanwhile, heat the butter and oil in a large, deep frying pan over a low to moderate heat. Add the garlic, chilli and tomatoes, turn the heat up to high and cook for about 30 seconds. Add the crab, turn the heat up again if possible and then add the vermouth and parsley. Cook quickly for about 30 seconds. Season generously with salt and pepper.

4 Add the pasta to the boiling water and cook for about 30 seconds. Drain thoroughly and transfer to the frying pan, tossing well to mix.

5 Serve immediately with a mixed green salad and wedges of lemon.

....

COOK'S TIP: Always try to use organic, free-range eggs when making pasta, as the bright yellow yolks will produce a brightly coloured yellow dough, which keeps its colour even when allowed to dry before cooking.

POTTED CHEESE WITH GUINNESS

This starter can be prepared in no time at all and then chilled and forgotten in the fridge while you get on with other things! It features the wonderful combination of rich Guinness and sharp Cheddar with an acidic creaminess that marries the flavours together.

1 Use the flat beater to cream the butter until really soft.

2 Attach the Rotary Slicer and Shredder and position the mixer bowl under it. Grate the cheese coarsely into the bowl, add all the remaining ingredients and mix again with the flat beater.

3 Pack the mixture into a small bowl or ramekin and smooth the surface, then cover and refrigerate for at least two hours.

4 Remove from the refrigerator 20 minutes before serving to soften a little and run a knife around the mixture to loosen the edge. Turn out and garnish with parsley. Spread on Spring Onion Soda Bread (see page 37) or serve with crackers.

SERVES 4
PREPARATION TIME: 10 minutes
CHILLING TIME: 2 hours

75 g butter
225 g grated strong Cheddar cheese, preferably Irish
2 Tbsp soured cream
4 Tbsp Guinness®
4 drops Tabasco
2 Tbsp finely chopped parsley, plus extra for garnishing
Freshly ground black pepper to taste (you should not need salt – there's enough in the cheese)

AUBERGINE DIP

SERVES 6 TO 8
PREPARATION TIME: 10 minutes
COOKING TIME: 45 minutes,
   plus cooling time

2 medium aubergines
Lemon juice (see method)
About 250 g ricotta cheese
8 halves oil-packed sun-dried
   tomatoes, drained and
   finely chopped
1 clove garlic, crushed
12 green or black olives,
   stoned and roughly
   chopped
4 Tbsp finely grated fresh
   Parmesan cheese
2 to 3 Tbsp freshly chopped
   parsley
Salt and freshly ground black
   pepper to taste

This dish is fresh, flavourful and creamy – ideal as a dip, a topping for bruschettas or tortillas, or served over a crisp salad. Add six to eight finely chopped anchovy fillets for a punchier flavour, if you wish.

1 Preheat the oven to 220°C/Gas Mark 7. Prick the aubergines and bake for 40 minutes until the skins are blackened and wrinkled and the flesh is soft. Cover with a wet teatowel and leave to cool for 10 to 15 minutes. Peel the aubergines by pulling the skin off from the bottom end up to the stalk and then quickly plunge them into cold water, to which a squeeze of lemon juice has been added, until completely cold.

2 Beat the ricotta in the mixer with the flat beater, then add the aubergine cut into rough chunks. Beat on a low speed until smooth, then add the remaining ingredients and mix gently to combine. Season to taste, then scoop into a bowl to serve.

COOK'S TIP: Adding lemon juice to the water prevents the peeled aubergines from discolouring.

SPRING ONION BREAD

A fabulously simple and quick soda bread that is ideal with cheese or soup for an informal lunch or a light dinner.

1 Preheat the oven to 220°C/Gas Mark 7 and lightly butter a baking tray.

2 Rub the butter into the flours, salt and baking soda using the flat beater. Add the chopped spring onions and mix again.

3 Add the buttermilk and mix slowly, just long enough to form a dough; do not over-mix or the bread will be heavy.

4 Knead lightly by hand on a floured surface, just enough to shape the dough into a round about 4 cm thick. Any loose mix left in the bowl should be dumped out and incorporated at this stage. Place on the baking tray and, with a sharp knife, score the bread, marking it into six pieces (do not cut all the way through).

5 Bake for 20 to 25 minutes until golden brown and set in the centre. Cool on a wire rack and break or slice the bread into pieces before serving.

SERVES 3 TO 4, MAKES 1 MEDIUM LOAF
PREPARATION TIME: 15 minutes
COOKING TIME: 20 to 25 minutes

25 g butter
150 g wholemeal flour
100 g plain flour
½ tsp salt
½ tsp baking soda
3 spring onions, trimmed and finely chopped
200 ml/¾ cup buttermilk

SPICY GREEN PAPAYA AND VEGETABLE SALAD

SERVES 2

PREPARATION TIME: 30 minutes

1 medium green papaya,
   peeled and quartered, seeds
   removed

½ cucumber, cut in half
   lengthways, seeds removed

2 carrots, peeled

2 Tbsp chopped unsalted and
   roasted peanuts

2 garlic cloves, finely chopped

3 to 5 green chillies, to taste

1 Tbsp sugar

1½ Tbsp lime juice

1 Tbsp Thai fish sauce

15 cooked prawns (optional)

4 fine green beans, ends
   removed and broken into
   2.5-cm pieces

4 cherry tomatoes, halved

1 Tbsp finely chopped flat-leaf
   parsley

3 mint leaves, finely chopped

This salad has the wonderful taste of Asia and is bursting with invigorating flavours and fragrances. You must use green, unripe papaya (the inside will be white) but, if you are unable to find this, leave the papaya out altogether and use cucumber (seeds removed) and carrot (peeled), or a mixture of both, instead. A ripe papaya will simply turn to mush used in this recipe!

1 First, grate the papaya and vegetables using the Rotary Slicer and Shredder fitted with the coarse shredding drum, then cover and set aside.

2 Prepare the dressing. Mix half the peanuts, garlic and chillies in the bowl with the flat beater on the slowest speed for about three minutes, to really beat up the ingredients. Then, with the motor still running at slow speed, add the remaining ingredients, ending with the grated vegetables. Mix until thoroughly combined.

3 Serve on a large platter with the remaining peanuts sprinkled over the top of the salad.

VEGETABLE FRITTERS WITH FETA AND MIXED SALAD LEAVES

This dish is ideal for lunch or as a light snack. Or, why not make mini-fritters for parties or snacks?

1 Preheat the oven to 180°C/Gas Mark 4. Coarsely grate the vegetables using the Rotary Slicer and Shredder. Catch them in a colander and squeeze them hard with your hands to remove as much liquid as possible.

2 Whisk together the spices, coriander, cornflour and egg in the mixer bowl, then season to taste with salt and pepper. Add the vegetables and mix well by hand, ensuring that all the vegetables are well coated in the batter.

3 Shape the mixture into eight round patties. Heat a small amount of oil (about 1 cm deep) in a large non-stick frying pan over a moderate heat and cook the fritters in batches until golden brown on both sides. You may have to add more oil during the cooking process. Transfer the fritters to a lightly oiled baking tray and bake for 5 minutes.

4 Serve two fritters on each plate topped with a handful of leaves and a sprinkling of crumbled feta.

COOK'S TIP: This dish is great with a really generous spoonful of caramelised onions – use 750 g of onions and follow the method on page 72. Crumbled blue cheese is delicious in this dish if you are not a feta fan.

SERVES 4
PREPARATION TIME: 20 minutes
COOKING TIME: 20 minutes

- 1 medium courgette, halved and seeds removed
- 1 medium sweet potato
- 1 medium onion
- 2 tsp ground coriander
- 2 tsp ground cumin
- 1 tsp paprika
- 4 Tbsp chopped fresh coriander
- 100 g cornflour
- 2 eggs, lightly beaten
- Salt and freshly ground black pepper to taste
- Oil for cooking
- 200 g feta cheese, crumbled (if using a marinated cheese, drain it thoroughly)
- Mixed salad leaves to serve

MID-WEEK
MEALS

In selecting our recipes for this chapter we have tried to keep preparation time to no more than about 30 minutes, a reasonable amount of time to spend in the kitchen while working and running a home too. Cooking times vary, but the family-style dishes are all contemporary and full of flavour.

SWEET POTATO AND ROASTED NUT LOAF

SERVES 4 TO 6

PREPARATION TIME: 20 minutes

COOKING TIME: I hour

50 g cashew nuts, roughly
    chopped

50 g pistachio nuts, roughly
    chopped

25 g sunflower seeds

25 g pumpkin seeds

I large onion, diced

I Tbsp olive oil

2 cloves garlic, finely chopped

2 tsp paprika

2 tsp cumin powder

I tsp chilli powder (optional)

2 eggs, beaten

2 Tbsp soured cream

I medium (approx 250 g)
    sweet potato, grated using
    the coarse shredder

I large apple, peeled, cored
    and grated using the coarse
    shredder

5 Tbsp flat-leaf parsley, finely
    chopped

50 g fresh breadcrumbs

Salt and freshly ground black
    pepper to taste

The fact that this loaf is so tasty makes it being full of healthy ingredients an added bonus, rather than the main selling point! Serve with dressed mixed salad leaves or freshly cooked baby vegetables (smothered in butter if the healthy angle is not uppermost in your mind!)

I Begin by roasting the nuts and seeds, keeping the pumpkin seeds separate from the others. This is a very important step and worth the effort, as their flavour will be hugely improved after roasting. Preheat the oven to 200°C/Gas Mark 6. Spread the nuts and seeds out on a baking tray and roast in the oven for about 10 minutes or until they start to become golden. Remove and allow to cool. Reduce the temperature of the oven to 190°C/Gas Mark 5. Oil a 450-g loaf tin.

2 Cook the onion in the olive oil over a low heat for about 10 minutes or until soft, then add the garlic and cook for another two minutes. Add the spices, salt and pepper, stir, cook for another minute and then remove the pan from the heat.

3 Beat the eggs and soured cream together in the mixing bowl with the flat beater, then add the remaining ingredients, including all the nuts other than the pumpkin seeds, and combine on the slowest setting mixing briefly.

4 Spread the pumpkin seeds evenly over the bottom of the prepared tin and then spoon the mixture in on top of them. Smooth the surface and bake for one hour.

5 Let the loaf cool in the tin for five minutes before turning out onto a serving dish and slicing. Serve hot or cold.

GARDEN PIZZA

This tasty pizza is a modern interpretation of an Italian classic and uses wonderfully young and tender baby vegetables for ultimate sweetness in flavour and crispness in texture. Your mixer makes light work of the dough.

SERVES 4 VERY GENEROUSLY
PREPARATION TIME: 40 minutes,
including proofing time
COOKING TIME: 25 to 30 minutes

FOR THE PIZZA DOUGH:
500 g plain flour
I tsp salt
I Tbsp easy blend dry yeast
I Tbsp olive oil
350 ml/I ½ cups warm water

FOR THE TOPPING:
2 Tbsp olive oil, plus more for
**   drizzling**
I large red onion, finely sliced
3 garlic cloves, finely chopped
250 g baby spinach leaves
Salt and freshly ground black
**   pepper to taste**
8 baby asparagus, halved
**   lengthways**
4 baby leeks, halved lengthwise
I courgette, cut into 5-cm
**   spears**
75 g green peas (from frozen if
**   necessary)**
Iced water (see method)
50 g mozzarella cheese, sliced
50 g ricotta cheese
2 Tbsp freshly grated
**   Parmesan cheese**
4 Tbsp finely chopped flat-leaf
**   parsley**
I Tbsp finely chopped chives
12 black olives, stoned
Rocket, dressed with olive oil
**   and lemon juice, for**
**   garnishing**

I First make the pizza dough. Combine the flour, salt and yeast in the mixer bowl using the dough hook. Add the olive oil, then gradually add the warm water to make a soft, manageable dough. Continue kneading on a medium setting for about five minutes until the dough is smooth and elastic. Form into the desired shape (see Cook's tip below) and cover loosely with a damp cloth or clingfilm. Leave the dough for about 40 minutes to rise.

2 Make the spinach topping while the dough is proofing. Heat the olive oil over low heat in a large saucepan. Add the onions and cook for five minutes, then add the garlic and cook for another five minutes, stirring frequently. Add the spinach and cover to allow the leaves to wilt, cooking about five more minutes. Season very generously with salt and pepper and allow to cool slightly. Blanch the remaining vegetables in boiling water for about one minute and then quickly immerse in a bowl of iced water, drain and set aside.

3 Preheat the oven to 220°C/Gas Mark 7. Drizzle olive oil over the risen pizza dough, spread with the spinach mixture and top with the remaining ingredients, which should be evenly distributed over the whole pizza. Drizzle more olive oil over the topping and bake for 25 to 30 minutes, or until the dough and the cheeses are golden.

4 Serve sliced with rocket leaves dressed in olive oil and lemon juice piled high on top of each portion.

COOK'S TIP: We like to make one large rectangular pizza in a baking tray for ease of handling and cooking, but you can divide the dough in half and make circular pizzas with 30-cm diameters, if you prefer. The dough also freezes well if you don't wish to use it all at once.

CELERIAC, BACON AND BLUE CHEESE GRATIN

This dish is ideal for mid-week meals as it is so versatile. Simply interchange these ingredients with those that you have available at the time. For example, almost any root vegetable can be used in place of celeriac, and other cooked meats, ham and cheeses (such as strong Cheddar, or nutty Gruyère) can also be substituted. Celeriac is also known as celery root.

....

1 Preheat the oven to 220°C/Gas Mark 7.

2 Attach the Rotary Slicer and Shredder and, with the coarse shredding drum, grate the bread to form crumbs and set aside. Then, using the shredding drum again, grate the celeriac into a large saucepan. Add the water to the pan, cover and "steam" for about five minutes. Meanwhile, cook the bacon in the sunflower oil so it just begins to crisp.

3 Drain excess liquid from the celeriac if there is any. Then, while it is still warm, add the butter, soured cream, mustard, thyme and lots of salt and pepper, and mix well until the butter has melted.

4 Pour the celeriac mixture into a small casserole or gratin dish. Sprinkle the bacon and any remaining oil over the top for flavour, then dot with three-quarters of the cheese, followed by the breadcrumbs. Top with the remaining cheese. Bake for 15 minutes or until golden brown.

SERVES 4 TO 6
PREPARATION TIME: 25 minutes
COOKING TIME: 15 minutes

- 100 g stale (or minimum 1 day old) bread
- 1 large (approx 800 g) celeriac, peeled and cut into manageable pieces
- 250 ml/1 cup water
- 100 g (approx 6 rashers) good-quality bacon, cut into 1-cm pieces
- 1 Tbsp sunflower or vegetable oil
- 50 g butter
- 140 ml/½ cup soured cream
- 2 tsp dried mustard
- 1 tsp dried thyme
- Salt and freshly ground black pepper to taste
- 100 g blue cheese (e.g. Stilton, Danish Blue), diced

ASIAN STYLE CRAB CAKES WITH MANGO AND AVOCADO SAMBAL

These crab cakes have a real taste of Asian flavour and are fantastic when topped with the accompanying sambal.

1 Prepare the sambal. Chop the mango and avocado into 6-mm dice, then add the remaining ingredients and mix well. Set aside until needed.

2 Mix all the crab cake ingredients together except the egg white, cornflour, sunflower oil and sesame oil (if using) with the flat beater at a slow speed. Transfer to another bowl, wash the mixer bowl and change the beater for the wire whip.

3 Whisk the egg white and cornflour together on high speed until white and fluffy but not firm. Fold the egg whites gently into the crab mixture using a metal spoon, ensuring that it is well blended.

4 Form the mixture into four large, round patties, or into 16 miniature ones. Cook in about 1 cm of oil for about two minutes on each side (miniature cakes will take less time, about one minute) or until golden. Serve immediately with the mango and avocado sambal and lime quarters.

SERVES 4
PREPARATION TIME: 15 minutes
COOKING TIME: 10 minutes

FOR THE MANGO AND AVOCADO SAMBAL:
½ ripe mango
1 ripe avocado
1 spring onion, finely chopped
1 small birds eye chilli, or Thai chilli, seeds removed and finely chopped
1 tsp Thai fish sauce
2 Tbsp lime juice
½ tsp sugar
1 Tbsp finely chopped fresh coriander
½ Tbsp finely chopped fresh parsley

FOR THE CRAB CAKES:
250 g white crab meat, well drained
2 spring onions, including green tops, finely chopped
2 Tbsp finely chopped fresh coriander
2 tsp lime juice
1 tsp light soy sauce
1 tsp Thai fish sauce
1 whole red birds eye chilli, or Thai chilli, finely chopped
1 stalk lemon grass, finely chopped
1 tsp fresh ginger, finely chopped
1 large egg white
1 Tbsp cornflour
Sunflower or vegetable oil for shallow frying
1 Tbsp sesame oil (optional)

LAMB AND ROSEMARY CLAFOUTIS

SERVES 4

PREPARATION TIME: 15 minutes

COOKING TIME: 40 to 45
   minutes

FOR THE BATTER:

125 g plain flour

¼ tsp salt

1 egg, beaten

280 ml/1¼ cups milk

2 Tbsp roughly chopped fresh
   rosemary

4 lamb sirloin steaks, 100g
   each

30 g plain flour

Salt and freshly ground black
   pepper to taste

4 Tbsp sunflower or vegetable
   oil

This recipe is a twist on the traditional toad-in-the-hole, usually made from Yorkshire Pudding batter that puffs up around a sausage, and the French classic clafoutis which is traditionally made with cherries as a dessert. Our version is easy to make and serves four very heartily.

1 Preheat the oven to 220 C/Gas Mark 7 and put a 1.5-litre baking dish into the oven to heat up.

2 Make the batter. Combine all the batter ingredients in the mixer bowl, and with the wire whip, whisk quickly to remove any lumps and ensure a smooth mixture.

3 Cut each steak in half lengthways. Then, put the flour, salt and pepper into a large plastic resealable bag, add the meat and shake until well coated. Heat the oil in a frying pan and quickly fry the meat so it begins to colour on each side. Pour the meat and oil into the hot baking dish and, working quickly, arrange the meat attractively, giving each piece its own space. Pour the batter over the meat and put it into the oven immediately.

4 Bake for 40 to 45 minutes or until the batter has risen and is golden in colour. Serve immediately with green vegetables and onion gravy.

COOK'S TIP: To make onion gravy, simply fry three to four finely sliced onions in a little sunflower oil and butter, over a low heat, until caramelised and golden in colour (about 10 minutes). Add a teaspoon of brown sugar, a splash of red wine and some gravy browning (according to manufacturer's instructions). Season to taste and whisk in 1 teaspoon of mustard, and 1 tablespoon of redcurrant jelly if liked. Bring to the boil, mixing continuously, then allow to cool slightly before serving.

TURKEY, HAM AND EGG PIE

This is a real favourite with us, and a great way of using up leftover turkey after Christmas. However, as cooked chicken is readily available in supermarkets and grocery stores, there's no excuse for this pie not to be a regular on the family menu.

1 Preheat the oven to 200°C/Gas Mark 6 and lightly butter a pie dish.

2 Make the sauce. Place the milk, flour and butter in a pan and heat gently, stirring constantly, until combined and bubbling. Continue to cook for one minute and then season with salt and pepper to taste. Transfer to a bowl and allow to cool slightly.

3 Make the pastry. Rub the butter into the flour with the pinch of salt on a slow speed (using the flat beater) until the mixture resembles fine breadcrumbs. Add enough cold water to make a firm dough, then transfer to a lightly floured surface and knead lightly. Roll out to fit the prepared pie dish.

4 For the filling, mix the cooked meats, hard-boiled eggs and capers into the sauce, then pour into the pie dish. Cover the filling with the pastry, crimping the edges and making a slit in the centre of the crust to allow the steam to escape.

5 Bake the pie for 30 minutes until golden brown. Serve hot or cold.

SERVES 4
PREPARATION TIME: 30 minutes
COOKING TIME: 30 minutes

FOR THE SAUCE:
425 ml/1³/₄ cups milk
4 Tbsp plain flour
50 g butter
Salt and freshly ground black
    pepper to taste

FOR THE PASTRY:
100 g butter
200 g plain flour
Pinch of salt
Cold water (see method)

FOR THE FILLING:
200 g cooked turkey, diced
200 g cooked ham, diced
2 large hard-boiled eggs,
    peeled and chopped
2 to 3 Tbsp small capers

HOME-MADE BURGERS

SERVES 4 (MAKES 4 BURGERS)
PREPARATION TIME: 15 minutes
COOKING TIME: 4 to 8 minutes
   (rare to well-done)

500 g good-quality steak
½ tsp sea salt
**½ tsp freshly ground black
   pepper (or green
   peppercorns, which are a
   great alternative)**
**1 small onion, finely grated
   (optional)**
**Oil for shallow frying if using a
   frying pan**

We prefer to use really good-quality meat for our burgers and so add few extra ingredients to get the full flavour of the meat. The benefit of mincing the meat yourself is that you can choose the cut of meat and will know exactly how much fat is in the resulting mince. Select a good-quality cut such as rump, sirloin or topside.

1 Cut the meat into strips and then process using the food grinder. You can use either the fine or coarse grinding plate depending on personal taste, but we prefer the coarse plate for texture. However, if you are using a poorer cut of meat, you may find that the fine plate produces a more tender result.

2 Combine the meat with the other ingredients and mix well using the flat beater. Shape into four rounds, each about 2 cm thick.

3 Heat a large, nonstick frying pan over medium heat, add the burgers and cook for 2 minutes each side for rare, or 4 minutes per side for well done, turning once. Alternatively, grill or barbecue for 6 to 8 minutes, turning only once.

4 Serve the burgers as they are, or in buns topped with lettuce; a slice of Roquefort cheese; a little crispy bacon and avocado; fried mushrooms and Swiss cheese; or capers and soured cream.

VARIATIONS:

Mince best cuts of lamb and combine with:

- Chopped dried apricots and ground cumin and coriander
- Grated parsnip and a little curry powder
- Chopped mint leaves and unsweetened yoghurt

Mince best cuts of pork and combine with:

- Grated apple and sage
- Redcurrants and parsley

Mince chicken breast and combine with:

- Thai spices
- Grated lemon zest and thyme
- Chopped sun-dried tomatoes and basil leaves

COOK'S TIP: Shape the meat with wet hands to prevent the mixture from sticking to your skin.

TACO BAKE

This is Tex–Mex meets comfort food! Here, spicy minced beef is rolled in cheesy scone dough and baked, making a filling dinner for an active family. Serve with freshly cooked vegetables or a tomato and avocado salad.

1 Brown the minced beef in a nonstick frying pan, then stir in the seasoning or spices and cook for another minute. Add the water and simmer for 20 minutes.

2 Preheat the oven to 200°C/Gas Mark 6. Rub the butter into the flour and salt in the mixer using the flat beater. Mix in most of the cheese and then add the milk and mix on a slow speed to make a soft, manageable dough.

3 Turn the dough out onto a lightly floured surface and roll it into a rectangular shape the same length as a large loaf tin. Spoon the beef down the centre of the dough. Working from the long side, roll the dough over the beef, encasing it inside the dough. Place in the lightly oiled loaf tin and scatter the remaining cheese over the top.

4 Bake for 30 minutes.

COOK'S TIP: For a creamy, cooling sauce to serve with the Bake, mix equal quantites of yoghurt and soured cream, then add grated lemon rind and juice to taste, with chopped parsley, salt and pepper.

SERVES 4 TO 6
PREPARATION TIME : 30 minutes
COOKING TIME : 25 to 30 minutes

500 g minced beef
Packet taco seasoning mix, or
   2 Tbsp chilli powder and
   1 tsp ground cumin
250 ml/1 cup water
50 g butter
250 g self-raising flour
Pinch of salt
50 g Cheddar cheese, grated
Milk to mix (see method)

QUICHE LORRAINE

SERVES 4
PREPARATION TIME: 25 minutes
COOKING TIME: 45 minutes

100 g butter, cut into cubes

200 g plain flour

Pinch of salt

Cold water to mix (see method)

1 small onion, very finely chopped

4 rashers good-quality bacon, finely chopped

3 eggs, beaten

425 ml/1³/₄ cups milk, or milk and light cream mixed

75 g Gruyère cheese, finely grated

Salt and freshly ground black pepper to taste

Nothing beats the mouth-watering taste of a well-baked quiche, with home-made pastry and a lightly set filling of cream and eggs with hints of cheese and bacon. Always use a metal baking dish to bake your quiche – china dishes will not allow the pastry to cook properly.

1 Place a baking tray in the oven and preheat to 220°C/Gas Mark 7

2 Prepare the pastry. Blend the butter into the flour and salt on a low speed, using the flat beater, until well blended. Add enough cold water to make a firm dough. Turn out onto a floured surface, knead lightly, roll out and use to line a 20-cm flan tin, about 4 cm deep.

3 Cook the onion and bacon together for five minutes over a gentle heat in a nonstick frying pan. Spoon into the flan tin.

4 Beat the eggs into the milk, or milk and cream, in a large bowl (using the mixer, or by hand), then add most of the cheese with some salt and pepper and beat again. Pour the mixture over the bacon and onion and scatter the remaining cheese on top.

5 Place the quiche on the hot baking tray and bake for 10 minutes. Lower the oven to 190°C/Gas Mark 5 and continue baking for another 30 to 35 minutes, until the filling is just set.

6 Allow to cool slightly before cutting. Serve the quiche warm or cold.

MEDITERRANEAN FISH PIE WITH CORNMEAL AND PARMESAN CRUST

A pie packed full of delicious seafood and topped with a crisp and unusual crust – this is a real favourite of ours.

1 First make the crust. Rub the butter into the cornmeal, flour and Parmesan cheese using the flat beater until the mixture resembles breadcrumbs. Add the beaten egg and yolk and mix to form a soft dough. Cover and chill in the refrigerator until needed.

2 Preheat the oven to 220°C/Gas Mark 7. Gently cook onion in the olive oil over a low heat for approximately five minutes. Add the garlic, aubergine and pepper and cook for a minute or two longer. Stir in the paprika and parsley, and then turn up the heat and add the sherry. Stir continuously until the sherry virtually evaporates and then add the remaining ingredients (except the egg for glazing). Stir carefully, reduce the heat and simmer for five minutes. Pour into a deep dish or pie plate about 20 × 7 cm (about 1.5 litres in volume).

3 Roll out the chilled cornmeal dough to fit the pie plate – it should be about 6 mm thick. Use extra cornmeal to prevent it from sticking to the worktop. Decorate the edges of the crust with a knife or your fingers, then brush with beaten egg and sprinkle with extra grated Parmesan cheese. Bake for 10 to 15 minutes, until golden, then serve immediately.

COOK'S TIP: To economise, try using inexpensive fish fillets such as haddock, or ask your fishmonger for a bag of mixed end cuts which often contains fabulous fish at a fraction of the price.

SERVES 4 TO 6
PREPARATION TIME: 25 minutes
COOKING TIME: 10 to15 minutes

FOR THE CRUST:
100 g butter, cut into small pieces
100 g cornmeal
40 g plain flour
50 g finely grated Parmesan cheese, plus extra to finish
1 egg, beaten
1 egg yolk

FOR THE FILLING:
1 Tbsp olive oil
1 large red onion, roughly chopped
2 large cloves garlic, finely sliced
1 medium aubergine, cut into 1.5-cm dice
1 large red pepper, cut into 1.5-cm dice
½ tsp paprika
2 large handfuls flat-leaf parsley, chopped
2 Tbsp dry sherry
400-g can chopped tomatoes
100 ml/½ cup water
½ tsp salt
2 tsp Demerara sugar
Few drops Tabasco (optional)
250 g fresh mixed prepared shellfish (e.g. mussels, prawns, squid, clams)
250 g thick cod fillets, skinned and diced in chunks
1 egg for glazing

CREAMY FISH BAKE

SERVES 4

PREPARATION TIME: 15 minutes

COOKING TIME: 45 minutes

200 g cream cheese

250 ml/1 cup soured cream

150 ml/⅔ cup milk

3 eggs

1 to 2 Tbsp horseradish,
  or 1 tsp wasabi

Salt and freshly ground black
  pepper to taste

About 500 g smoked mackerel
  or smoked trout

6 to 8 spring onions, trimmed
  and sliced

6 to 8 slices ciabatta

Paprika for garnishing

Mix this up in next to no time, and then take the time to relax while this delicious fish bake is in the oven. We like using smoked mackerel or smoked trout, but you could try smoked haddock or cod as an alternative.

1 Preheat the oven to 190°CC/Gas Mark 5 and lightly butter a large gratin dish.

2 Beat the cream cheese and soured cream until smooth in the mixer using the flat beater, then add the milk, eggs, horseradish and salt and pepper and beat again.

3 Skin the mackerel and break into large flakes, then add it to the bowl along with the spring onions and mix to combine on a slow speed.

4 Line the sides of the dish with 1-cm slices of the bread, then pour in the mackerel cream. Sprinkle a little paprika over the top and bake for 45 minutes, or until set. Serve immediately.

CARROT AND CORIANDER SOUFFLE

SERVES 3

PREPARATION TIME: 20 minutes

COOKING TIME: 40 to 45
  minutes

50 g butter

50 g plain flour

1 Tbsp ground coriander

½ tsp ground turmeric

250 ml/1 cup milk

6 eggs, separated

2 to 3 carrots, finely grated

2 Tbsp chopped coriander

Salt and freshly ground black
  pepper to taste

Don't let the thought of making a soufflé be a worry – just think of it as white sauce with egg whites folded in! Quick to make, light and very tasty, this is a perfect mid-week munch, especially if you are tired and eating late and don't want anything too heavy.

1 Preheat the oven to 180°C/Gas Mark 4. Lightly butter a 20-cm soufflé dish (about 1.5-litres/6 cups capacity).

2 Melt the butter in a large pan, add the flour and spices and beat well. Cook over low heat for one minute or so, then gradually add the milk, beating well after each addition. The mixture will be very thick. Cook for another minute, stirring constantly, and then cool slightly.

3 Add the egg yolks and beat thoroughly, then stir in the grated carrots, coriander and salt and pepper to taste.

4 Meanwhile, whisk the egg whites with the wire whip until very stiff, starting slowly and then increasing the speed. Fold the whipped egg whites into the carrot mixture, a little at a time, using a metal spoon. Scrape the mixture into the prepared dish and bake for 40 to 45 minutes until set. Serve immediately.

CHORIZO AND MOZZARELLA STUFFED MUSHROOMS

These mushrooms are ideal for a mid-week meal, as they are incredibly quick and easy to make. They use ingredients that are very easy to come by, or that you might well have in the refrigerator or pantry.

1 Preheat the oven to 200°C/Gas Mark 6. Grease a baking tray.

2 Wipe each mushroom clean with a damp cloth and carefully remove the stems, setting them aside. Place each mushroom on the prepared baking tray, stem-side up. Divide the spinach equally among the mushrooms, making sure that no spinach sticks out over the edges.

3 Grate the mushroom stalks, bread, garlic, mozzarella cheese and chorizo into the mixer bowl using the fine shredding drum on the Rotary Slicer and Shredder. Add the thyme, chilli flakes (if using) and a generous amount of salt and pepper and mix thoroughly with the flat beater. Pile the mixture onto the mushrooms and press down gently with the palm of your hand. Drizzle with olive oil, scatter Parmesan cheese over and bake for 10 to 15 minutes. Serve with a large salad and new potatoes or warmed crusty bread.

COOK'S TIP: Instead of chorizo and mozzarella, use other cooked meats or hams (preferably with a strong flavour) and any cheese that melts well. Rocket or other young greens can be used in place of spinach and the herbs can be varied, too.

SERVES 4
PREPARATION TIME: 10 to 15 minutes
COOKING TIME: 10 to 15 minutes

4 large portabello mushrooms
Small handful baby spinach leaves
100 g (about 4 slices) stale bread, minimum 1 day old
1 clove garlic, peeled
About 125 g mozzarella cheese
50 g smoked chorizo sausage
1 Tbsp fresh thyme
Pinch chilli flakes (optional)
Salt and freshly ground black pepper to taste
2 Tbsp olive oil
Grated Parmesan cheese to sprinkle over the top

EASY ENTERTAINING

Is there such a thing? Well, with a table mixer to do the major mixing jobs for you, there certainly is! Guests are always bowled over by home-made food, and our selection of dishes yields fabulous results without too much effort. There's a mixture of chef-inspired, stylish dishes that are straightforward when following our directions, as well as some more relaxed dishes for informal, "kitchen table" dinners.

LOBSTER RAVIOLI WITH SPARKLING ROSE AND PINK PEPPERCORN SAUCE

ERVES 4

PREPARATION TIME: 2 hours and
   20 minutes

COOKING TIME: 1 to 2 minutes

FOR THE STOCK:

2 shallots, diced

1 carrot, diced

1 celery stalk, diced

1 leek, diced

1 bouquet garni (tie some
   thyme, parsley and a bay leaf
   to half a celery stick with
   string)

Juice of half a lemon

1 litre/4 cups water

Shell from 1 lobster

FOR THE FILLING:

Tail and claw meat from
   1 small cooked lobster
   (about 450 g), shell reserved
   for stock

140 ml/½ cup double cream

1 egg, beaten

Pinch of cayenne pepper

Salt and freshly ground black
   pepper to taste

This dish is very special and well worth the effort. Don't be put off by the seemingly complicated nature of the recipe or the time involved in making it. Each step is actually very easy to follow, and much of the time is simply due to slow cooking or cooling as opposed to hard work! The final dish need not be expensive either, because despite the initial outlay for the lobster, making the pasta and sauce yourself makes this an economical option for entertaining.

1 Begin by making the stock. Put all the ingredients into a large pan and bring to the boil, then reduce the heat and simmer for one hour. It will have reduced by a quarter. Allow to cool completely, with the shell still in the stock.

2 Meanwhile, make the lobster filling. Finely chop the lobster meat. Using the wire whip, whip the cream until thick, add the egg and seasoning and whisk again before adding the lobster and combining carefully. Refrigerate until needed.

3 Begin the sauce by melting half the butter in a large saucepan and then adding the shallots. Cook for about 10 minutes over low heat, or until the shallots are translucent and soft. Add the rosé and reduce until the pan is almost dry. Turn off the heat and leave until needed.

4 When the stock is cool, drain it through a large sieve or colander, reserving the liquid and discarding the shells and vegetables. Add the stock to the sauce and bring it back to the boil before lowering the heat slightly and reducing by approximately two-thirds of its original volume. This will take about 20 to 30 minutes.

5 While the sauce is reducing, make the pasta dough. Use the dough hook to combine the ingredients until they come together. Fit the pasta maker and run the dough through the standard roller on the lowest setting at least 15 times, folding the dough back on itself between each rolling. Divide the dough into four and begin rolling each piece at setting 2, repeating the process at each

ascending setting until you reach setting 5. Lay the four pieces of dough out on a well-floured surface and cut into 7.5-cm wide strips with a sharp knife. You should have 20 rectangular strips.

6 Remove the lobster filling from the refrigerator. Put about 1 teaspoon of filling about 2.5-cm from the bottom end of each pasta strip. Use your finger to smooth a little water around each mound of filling and then fold the top of the strip down over it. Press down around the filling and seal firmly. Place each ravioli on a floured tray, cover and refrigerate while you finish the sauce.

7 When the sauce has been reduced, add the creme fraiche,, tomato purée and seasonings (except the basil leaves) and whisk in the remaining butter until melted and combined. Remove from the heat until needed.

8 When you are ready to eat, heat the sauce gently and bring a large pan of salted water to the boil. Drop the ravioli into the water and cook for about one to two minutes. Serve five ravioli per person on warmed plates and pour the hot sauce over the top. Scatter with the shredded basil and serve immediately.

FOR THE SAUCE:
50 g butter
2 shallots, finely chopped
250 ml/1 cup sparkling rosé brut
Fish stock (see opposite)
3 Tbsp creme fraiche
1 Tbsp tomato purée
1 tsp pink peppercorns
Pinch of cayenne pepper
Salt to taste
10 basil leaves, finely shredded

FOR THE PASTA DOUGH:
250 g plain flour
2 eggs
1 egg yolk

INDIVIDUAL WILD MUSHROOM AND THYME TARTS

Individual tarts look very attractive and professional and take only a small amount of extra effort. These tartlets are a fabulous starter, or equally wonderful as a light main course served with a large mixed green salad.

1 Make the pastry. Sieve the flour, salt and thyme together in the mixer bowl. Add the butter and mix using the flat beater at slow speed until the contents resemble breadcrumbs. Beat in the yolk and then the water, adding a tablespoon at a time (you may not need it all) until the mixture comes together as a dough. Wrap in kitchen foil or clingfilm and refrigerate for 30 minutes.

2 Meanwhile, preheat the oven to 200°C/Gas Mark 6. Grease six individual tart tins that have removable bottoms (10 x 2.5 cm).

3 Roll the pastry out on a floured surface to about 6-mm thickness. Using a 14-cm round pastry cutter, cut out six circles and line each tart tin with the pastry, pushing the dough down firmly into the edges of the tins. Remove any surplus pastry by passing a rolling pin over the top of each tin; this will also give you a professional finish. Prick the bases thoroughly with a fork and bake for 15 minutes or until lightly golden. Remove from the oven and reduce the temperature to 170°C/Gas Mark 3.

4 Meanwhile, make the filling. Melt the butter in a medium frying pan over medium heat. Add the mushrooms and sauté briefly before adding the garlic and stirring thoroughly. Allow the mushrooms to get a little brown as they cook, turning up the heat if necessary. Add the sherry and cook over a high heat until it has virtually evaporated, then add the thyme and stir well. Allow to cool slightly before dividing the mixture evenly among the tarts.

5 Beat together the eggs, soured cream and Parmesan cheese and pour the mixture into each tart, leaving about 6 mm of pastry showing at the top. Sprinkle with a little extra Parmesan cheese and bake for 30 to 40 minutes or until golden and set. Serve the tarts warm or cold, piled with rocket leaves dressed with balsamic vinegar.

SERVES 6
PREPARATION TIME: 30 minutes
COOKING TIME: 45 to 55 minutes

FOR THE PASTRY:
125 g plain flour
Pinch of salt
1 tsp dried thyme
50 g butter, chilled and diced
1 large egg yolk
2 Tbsp cold water

FOR THE FILLING:
25 g butter
200 g mixed shop-bought wild mushrooms, roughly chopped
2 cloves garlic, finely chopped
1 Tbsp dry sherry
1 tsp dried thyme
2 eggs, beaten
140 ml/½ cup soured cream
50 g fresh Parmesan cheese, finely grated, plus more for garnishing

STEAK, MUSHROOM AND OYSTER PIE

SERVES 4 TO 6

PREPARATION TIME: 2 hours 35 minutes, including chilling time for the pastry

COOKING TIME: 1½ to 2 hours

FOR THE ROUGH PUFF PASTRY:

250 g plain flour

¼ tsp salt

175 g butter

1 tsp lemon juice

About 4 Tbsp ice-cold water

FOR THE FILLING:

500 g boneless chuck or blade steak, trimmed and cut into 2-cm cubes

3 Tbsp seasoned flour (plain flour mixed with salt, pepper and 2 tsp mixed herbs)

2 medium onions, chopped

75 g whole baby button mushrooms, cleaned

12 oysters, freshly shucked with liquor reserved, or canned

1 Tbsp oyster sauce

4 Tbsp red wine

125 ml/½ cup reduced beef stock

1 beaten egg or milk for glazing

This British classic is just as tasty as it has always been. The method may seem very long-winded, but much of the time is spent chilling the pastry or slow-cooking the pie, so you can concentrate on preparing for your guests. Of course, if you have the pastry prepared already there is very little to be done. To make the reduced beef stock, simmer 250 ml/1 cup stock over a medium heat until half its original volume.

1 Make the pastry. Sieve the flour and salt into the mixer bowl and add the butter. Using the flat beater at a slow speed, roughly combine the ingredients; the butter should remain in lumps. Add the lemon juice and enough ice-cold water, a spoonful at a time, to make a soft, but very lumpy dough. Draw into a ball with your hands and place on a lightly floured surface.

2 Roll the dough out into a rectangular shape (about 25 × 15 cm). Then, fold the top third of the pastry over the middle third of the rectangle and the bottom third over that. Give the dough a 90-degree turn and roll out again to make the same size rectangle. Repeat the folding process. Cover in clingfilm and chill in the refrigerator for 30 minutes, then repeat rolling and folding as above. Do this – rolling, folding and chilling – four times in total, by which time the dough should be smooth. Cover and chill again until required.

3 Prepare the filling. In a plastic resealable bag, toss the steak in the seasoned flour until evenly covered. Transfer the meat to a 1-litre pie dish and add the onion, mushrooms and oysters. Mix well with your hands to ensure an even distribution of ingredients. If using fresh oysters, include the liquor at this time and exclude the oyster sauce. In a small bowl, mix the oyster sauce (if using), red wine and reduced stock together before pouring over the meat in the pie dish.

4 Preheat the oven to 230°C/Gas Mark 8. Roll the pastry out on a floured surface to about a 6-mm thickness. Cut a strip from the outside edge of the pastry. Moisten the edge of the pie dish with a little water and stick this strip to it. Trim off any excess. Moisten this strip before placing the rolled pastry over the pie dish. Seal and trim the edges before decorating, either by pinching them

with thumb and forefinger or by making indentations by pressing into them with the prongs of a fork. Make a small hole in the top of the pie to allow the steam to escape and decorate with the remaining pastry, if you wish. Brush with a little beaten egg or milk to glaze.

5 Bake the pie for 10 minutes or until the pastry has risen and is golden brown, then cover the pie with a loose "tent" of kitchen foil and lower the temperature to 180°CC/Gas Mark 4. Cook for another 1½ to 2 hours, or until the meat is tender when tested through the crust with a skewer. Serve immediately with fresh vegetables and creamy mashed potatoes.

SERVES 4 TO 6

**PREPARATION TIME: 2 hours
and 25 minutes, including
chilling time for the pastry**

**COOKING TIME: 30 to 35
minutes**

FOR THE CURRY PASTE:

1 large stalk lemon grass,
 finely chopped

2 Tbsp peeled and finely
 chopped root ginger

½ tsp finely chopped lime zest

4 small green chillies, finely
 chopped (with seeds if you
 like your curry hot)

3 garlic cloves, finely chopped

2 shallots, finely chopped

¼ tsp coriander seeds

¼ tsp cumin seeds

¼ tsp salt

¼ tsp ground turmeric

FOR THE ROUGH PUFF PASTRY:

250 g plain flour

¼ tsp salt

175 g butter

1 tsp lemon juice

Milk or beaten egg to glaze

FOR THE CURRY FILLING:

375 ml/1½ cups coconut milk

2 large boneless chicken
 breasts, thinly sliced

½ tbsp sugar

1 Tbsp Thai fish sauce

125 g aubergine, cut into
 1.5-cm cubes

125 g green beans, cut into
 2.5-cm lengths

3 kaffir lime leaves, torn into
 pieces with stems discarded

10 sweet basil leaves

THAI CHICKEN PIE

*East meets West! This pie combines a family favourite with exciting
Asian flavours.*

....

1 Make the pastry following the method on page 68 (Steak, Mushroom and
Oyster Pie). Cover in clingfilm and set aside in the refrigerator to chill for two
hours.

2 Make the curry paste. Put all the ingredients except the turmeric into the
mixer bowl and, using the flat beater, mix the ingredients at medium speed for
about 10 minutes or until a rough paste is achieved. You may need to stop the
machine intermittently to push the contents back into the bottom of the bowl.
Then, using a metal spoon, stir in the turmeric and set aside.

3 Next, make the filling. Put two spoonfuls of coconut milk into a wok or large
saucepan. Stir gently on a low heat until the coconut oil begins to separate
from the milk; this will be very obvious when it happens. Add the curry paste
and stir until there is a distinct smell of chillies (the best test is to sniff the
contents of the pan and if it makes you sneeze, then it's ready!) Add a little
more coconut milk if the pan has become too dry, and then add the chicken,
sugar and fish sauce. Stir until the chicken turns white, then pour in the rest of
the coconut milk. Turn up the heat a little and add the aubergine and beans.
Cook on a high heat for about five minutes to reduce the mixture and then
remove from the heat. Add the lime leaves and basil.

4 Preheat the oven to 200°C/Gas Mark 6. Divide the pastry in half and roll out
into two rectangles (about 30 x 20 cm). Lay one piece on a lightly floured
baking tray and spoon the chicken mixture over it, leaving about a 2.5-cm
border on all sides. Brush a little water around the edges and lay the second
rectangle of pastry over the top, squeezing the edges together and being sure to
seal the pastry thoroughly so there is no chance of the filling escaping. Use your
thumb and forefinger to flute the edge and make it look more attractive. Brush
with milk or beaten egg to glaze and cut two or three little holes in the top to
let the steam out.

5 Bake the pie for about 30 to 35 minutes, or until it has puffed up and is a rich
golden colour. Eat hot, or allow to cool.

ROASTED ONION TART WITH BALSAMIC VINEGAR

SERVES 6

PREPARATION TIME: 40
  minutes

COOKING TIME: 30 minutes

FOR THE FILLING:

750 g onions

6 whole cloves garlic, peeled

3 bay leaves

6 sprigs fresh thyme

Salt and freshly ground black
  pepper to taste

3 Tbsp olive oil

1 Tbsp balsamic vinegar

FOR THE BASE:

3 Tbsp sesame seeds

200 g plain flour

½ tsp salt

1 egg, beaten

3 Tbsp olive oil

Water to mix

Slow-cooked onions make a deliciously rich vegetable filling for numerous tarts and pies, and this is one of our favourite recipes. As an alternative to roasting, simmer the onions slowly for an hour or more. The filling can also be used by itself as an onion relish (see page 41). Use the best balsamic vinegar you can afford.

1 Preheat the oven to 220°C/Gas Mark 7. To make the filling, slice the onions into a large roasting tin using the Rotary Slicer and Shredder attachment and add the garlic, bay leaves and thyme. Season well with salt and pepper, drizzle with the olive oil and balsamic vinegar and toss to mix. Roast for 30 minutes, stirring once.

2 Meanwhile, prepare the base. Mix the sesame seeds with the flour and salt in the mixer bowl using the flat beater, then add the egg, oil and as little water as is necessary to make a firm dough. Lightly flour a baking tray and roll the base out on it to make about a 25-cm circle.

3 Season the onions again; they should be soft but not too brown. Scoop them onto the base, removing the herbs. Drizzle with a little more olive oil and balsamic vinegar and bake for 30 minutes.

FILLED SAVOURY BRIOCHE

MAKES 12 BRIOCHE, SERVES 6
**PREPARATION TIME: about 1½
    hours, including rising time**
COOKING TIME: 15 minutes

FOR THE BRIOCHE:
250 g plain flour
1 Tbsp easy blend dry yeast
3 Tbsp milk
100 g butter, melted
1 tsp caster sugar
½ tsp salt
2 eggs, beaten

FOR THE FILLING:
1 Tbsp olive oil
1 red onion, halved and sliced
1 clove garlic, finely chopped
**2 giant handfuls (about 250 g)
    baby spinach leaves**
50 g feta cheese, cubed
**12 oil-packed sun-dried
    tomatoes, drained**
**12 small marinated hot
    peppers**
12 stoned black olives

1 beaten egg or milk to glaze

These savoury brioche are perfect for entertaining at buffets, parties or picnics. They can be made with any filling you choose, and because they freeze well, they can be made in advance – although they are undoubtedly best eaten on the day they are baked. Keep the filling on the dry side and don't be tempted to be overly generous or it will just ooze out during cooking.

1 Make the brioche. Put all the ingredients into the mixer bowl and mix well with the dough hook for two to three minutes at a moderate speed. The dough will be rather sticky, but don't worry. Bring it together with your hands and allow it to rise in the mixer bowl covered with plastic film, in a warm place for 1 hour.

2 Meanwhile, make the filling. Heat the olive oil in a large pan and add the onion. Cook slowly for about eight minutes, then add the garlic and cook for another two minutes. Stir in the spinach, turn off the heat, cover and leave for about five minutes, or until the spinach is wilted. Set aside and allow to cool until needed.

3 Punch down the dough using the dough hook and knead again for about three minutes. Divide the dough into 12 balls and roll each one into a 10-cm circle. Put a tablespoon of the spinach into the centre of each, then add a cube of feta and one each of the sun-dried tomatoes, hot peppers and olives.

4 Preheat the oven to 230°C/Gas Mark 8. Moisten the edges of the dough with water or milk and gather the dough around the filling to form a ball. Place with the seams down on a baking tray and let rise for about 15 minutes.

5 Brush the tops with the egg or milk to glaze and bake for about 15 minutes until golden. Serve warm, or allow to cool completely and eat cold. Cool slightly before serving warm, as the filling will be very hot.

BAKED SPICED PORK TERRINE

A home-made terrine is a glorious starter – full of top-quality meat and spiced in a more adventurous way than a shop-bought pâté. Make two while you are in the mood and freeze one for later. It will keep for up to three months in great condition. Ask your butcher to provide you with pig's liver – if this is not available, chicken liver is a good alternative.

....

1 Preheat the oven to 180°C/Gas Mark 4. Line the base of two large loaf tins with baking parchment.

2 Stretch the bacon slices gently with the back of a knife, making them thinner as you pull. Use the stretched pieces to line the prepared tins, leaving the ends of the bacon dangling over the sides for now.

3 If necessary, remove the rind from the pork and cut the meat into long strips. Trim the liver and cut that into pieces of a similar size.

4 Heat a small frying pan until hot, then add the fennel seeds and dry-roast them for 30 seconds or so, until fragrant. Transfer to a mortar and pestle and grind, or crush them with the end of a rolling pin on a cutting board. Place the sausagemeat in the mixer bowl, break it up slightly with the flat beater and add the crushed fennel.

5 Set the food grinder fitted with the coarse plate onto the mixer. Mince the pork, liver and garlic into the bowl of sausagemeat, pressing the meat through with the stomper supplied. Add the crushed chilli, salt and pepper and mix well with the flat beater. Divide the mixture between the prepared tins, pressing it down evenly, then fold the bacon over the meat and cover the tins with kitchen foil.

6 Place the terrines in a small roasting tin, then fill the roasting tin with boiling water until it comes halfway up the sides of the terrines. Bake in the water bath in the oven for two hours, then allow to cool completely.

7 Press the terrines in the tins by placing heavy weights or tins filled with cans on the kitchen foil covering. Refrigerate with the weights overnight.

8 Loosen the terrines with a thin knife, then turn them out, scraping away any jelly and juices. Serve sliced with hot toast, gherkins, mustard or chutney.

MAKES 2, EACH SERVES 6 TO 8
PREPARATION TIME: 30 minutes
COOKING TIME: 2 hours, plus
  overnight chilling

12 streaky bacon rashers
About 1 kg boneless pork
  shoulder
About 350 g pig's liver
1 Tbsp fennel seeds
About 500 g pork
  sausagemeat
3 to 4 cloves garlic
1 Tbsp crushed chilli
1 tsp salt
1 tsp freshly ground black
  pepper

WATERCRESS ROULADE WITH VEGETABLE HUMMUS

SERVES 6 TO 8 AS A STARTER,
4 AS A MAIN COURSE
PREPARATION TIME: 30 minutes
COOKING TIME: 10 minutes

FOR THE ROULADE:
4 eggs
170 g watercress or rocket,
very finely chopped
2 Tbsp plain flour, sieved
½ tsp salt
½ tsp freshly ground black
pepper
Generous pinch of freshly
grated nutmeg

FOR THE FILLING:
5 spring onions, trimmed
1 red pepper
2 carrots, finely shredded
200 g prepared hummus
Salt and freshly ground black
pepper to taste

Stunningly colourful, light and full of flavour (besides being very quick to make), this is an ideal dish for easy entertaining. Serve warm or cold, with a simple salad garnish as a starter, or with a mixed salad and potatoes for a more substantial main course.

1 Preheat the oven to 220°C/Gas Mark 7. Line a Swiss-roll tin with baking parchment.

2 Whisk the eggs until very thick, starting slowly and gradually increasing the speed. This will take up to 10 minutes.

3 Meanwhile, chop the watercress very finely, then add the flour, salt, pepper and nutmeg, and toss together.

4 The eggs are ready when they are very thick and pale and the wire whip leaves a thick trail in the mixture. Add the watercress and whisk briefly to combine, slowly at first and then quickly for a few seconds. Do not over-mix.

5 Scrape the mixture into the prepared tin, gently level the top and bake for 10 minutes, until set and lightly browned.

6 Turn the roulade out onto a cooling rack lined with fresh baking parchment. Carefully remove the baked paper and make a shallow cut into one end of the roulade, about 2 cm from the edge. Roll the roulade up tightly with the paper inside to prevent it from sticking together. Leave and allow to cool for 10 minutes.

7 Finely chop the spring onions and red pepper, and then mix with the carrots and hummus, seasoning to taste.

8 Unroll the roulade, remove the paper and spread carefully with the filling. Roll again, this time using the paper on the outside just to keep the roulade firmly in shape.

9 Serve warm or cold, cut into 1-cm slices with a sharp, straight-bladed knife.

ROASTED LEMON AND SAFFRON CHICKEN LASAGNE

SERVES 6

PREPARATION TIME: 45 minutes

COOKING TIME: 1 hour and 35 minutes

FOR THE CHICKEN:

3 medium onions, each cut into 16 wedges

6 boneless chicken breasts, skin on (about 1 kg) and cut into wide strips

Large pinch saffron strands

6 garlic cloves, peeled and cut in half lengthways

Leaves from 4 sprigs of fresh rosemary, leaves removed and stems discarded

1 tsp sugar

2 lemons, quartered

60 ml/¼ cup olive oil

Salt and freshly ground black pepper to taste

250 ml/1 cup white wine

24 black olives, stoned

FOR THE PASTA:

250 g plain flour

2 eggs

1 egg yolk

Lasagne can always be counted on as a great dish for entertaining, but this version adds an element of luxury and a whole host of new flavours, colours and textures. Slow roasting the chicken with saffron and lemons makes a huge difference to the final outcome, adding lots of flavour.

1 Preheat the oven to 200°C/Gas Mark 6. Grease a large (1 to 1½ litres capacity) rectangular baking dish.

2 Place all the chicken ingredients except the wine in a roasting tin, squeeze the lemons over them and throw in the peel too! Mix thoroughly with your hands. Bake in the oven for 15 minutes and then add the wine, shaking the tin carefully to distribute the ingredients. Cook for another 25 minutes, shaking the tin once again during that time to ensure even cooking. Remove from the oven and allow to cool until needed. Reduce oven temperature to 180°C/Gas Mark 4.

3 Meanwhile, make the pasta. Combine the pasta ingredients with the dough hook at medium speed until they begin to form a ball. Bring the dough together with your hands.

4 Run the dough through the pasta maker roller on setting 1 a minimum of 15 times. Each time fold the dough back on itself before feeding it through the rollers again. When smooth and almost leathery to the touch, cut into four, and increase to setting 2 and run each piece through again. Repeat this process and gradually ascend the settings to number 4. Lay the four lengths out onto a lightly floured surface and cut into about sixteen 10-cm wide rectangles.

5 Bring a large pan of salted water to the boil. Fill a bowl or the sink with cold water and lay a clean tea towel on the worktop next to it. Drop the lasagne sheets into the boiling water three at a time and cook for about 30 seconds, then remove them using a slotted spoon and immediately drop them into the cold water to cool rapidly. Continue this process until all the lasagne sheets are cooked and cooled. Carefully lay each sheet on the tea towel, making sure they do not overlap. Lay another clean tea towel over the top and continue the process, finishing with another tea towel to prevent the pasta from drying out.

Leave until needed. The pasta will remain in reasonable condition like this for a few hours, but is undoubtedly better if used as soon as possible.

6 Make the béchamel sauce. Melt the butter for the sauce in a medium saucepan and then add the flour. Stir for two minutes, then gradually stir in the warm milk and continue stirring until the mixture thickens and bubbles slightly. Remove from the heat, season to taste with salt, white pepper and mustard.

7 To assemble the lasagne, spread half the chicken mixture over the base of the prepared baking dish and scatter with 12 olives. Layer half the pasta evenly over the meat and top with half the sauce. Then repeat the process finishing with a scattering of Parmesan cheese and dot with the diced butter. Bake for 45 minutes or until golden brown all over. Serve with a green salad or vegetables.

FOR THE BÉCHAMEL SAUCE:
50 g butter
2 heaped Tbsp plain flour
650 ml/2½ cups warmed milk
Salt and white pepper to
1 tsp dried mustard
24 stoned black olives
50 g Parmesan cheese
20 g butter, diced

SPICY LEEK AND SQUASH PATE

A vivid orange colour when made with butternut squash, this dip is a light starter with toast or vegetable crudités, or it can be served with a salad as a simple lunch. We find it to be a perfect late summer dish.

1 Slice the squash using the Rotary Slicer and Shredder attachment, catching the pieces in a colander or steamer basket. Steam until tender, about 15 minutes. Alternatively, cook the squash with a tablespoon or two of water in the microwave for about five minutes on high. Allow to cool.

2 Slice the leek in the same way. Heat the oil in a frying pan, add the leek, dried mustard and cayenne, and cook slowly for four to five minutes, until the leek is soft but not browned. Allow the leek to cool.

3 Beat the squash until smooth in the mixer bowl using the flat beater. Add the cream cheese and beat again, adding plenty of salt and pepper.

4 Finally, add the leeks and beat them into the mixture. Season to taste with salt and pepper again and then transfer to a serving dish. Chill for about 30 minutes, but do not serve too cold or you will inhibit the flavour of the dish. Garnish with chopped parsley.

SERVES 6
PREPARATION TIME: 45 minutes,
including cooling time
CHILLING TIME: 30 minutes

500 g peeled and deseeded
squash, such as butternut
1 large leek (about 200 g),
trimmed
2 Tbsp olive oil
½ tsp dried mustard
½ tsp cayenne pepper or chilli
powder
200 g cream cheese
Salt and freshly ground black
pepper to taste
Freshly chopped parsley for
garnishing

WARM GOAT'S CHEESE AND PARSNIP SOUFFLES

This is comfort food at its most glamorous! Here we unite two very distinctive flavours that act surprisingly well together. These soufflés are an ideal start to a meal, but just as good for entertaining as a lighter main course option.

....

1 Shred the parsnip using the coarse drum of the Rotary Slicer and Shredder, then steam in a covered steamer for five to ten minutes, or until soft. Remove and pat dry on kitchen paper. Mash well and set aside.

2 Preheat the oven to 200°C/Gas Mark 6. Grease six small pudding moulds or ramekins (about 200 ml each) and dust the insides with grated Parmesan cheese, shaking away any excess.

3 Combine the butter, flour and milk in a small saucepan and whisk continuously over a low heat until the mixture thickens. Remove from the heat and stir in the parsnip, egg yolks, goat's cheese and spices. Season to taste with salt and pepper.

4 Using the wire whip, whisk the egg whites until soft peaks form and then carefully fold into the parsnip mixture until just combined.

5 Divide the mixture evenly among the prepared moulds or ramekins, sprinkle with the remaining Parmesan cheese and bake for 20 minutes or until risen and golden in colour. Allow to cool for five minutes, by which time the soufflés will have dropped slightly. Use a knife to loosen the edges and turn out onto plates, bottom side up. Serve with mixed salad leaves.

SERVES 6
PREPARATION TIME: 30 minutes
COOKING TIME: 20 minutes

2 large parsnips (about 250 g), peeled
20 g Parmesan cheese, finely grated
50 g butter, diced
50 g plain flour
250 ml/1 cup milk
3 eggs, separated
100 g soft goat's cheese, chopped
Pinch of freshly grated nutmeg
Pinch of paprika
Salt and freshly ground black pepper to taste

CHEESE, APPLE AND COURGETTE FONDUE

The thing that deters most people from preparing a cheese fondue for a dinner party is grating the cheese. Well, your Rotary Slicer and Shredder will make short work of that. We have often found cheese fondues to be too rich, but the addition of chillies, apple and courgette makes a much lighter dish. Use mild to medium-hot chillies, according to your tastes.

....

1 Attach the Rotary Slicer and Shredder to your mixer with the fine shredding drum in place. Shred the shallots and chillies into a large saucepan, then change the drum to the coarse shredder. Shred the courgette and apple and add them to the pan with the white wine and lemon juice. Bring to the boil and cook for a minute or so. Remove from the heat.

2 Shred the cheeses straight into the saucepan and stir well. Return to the heat and cook slowly until the cheese has melted, stirring constantly.

3 Blend the cornflour with a little water or more wine, add it to the pan and cook for another three to four minutes until bubbling and thick. Season to taste with salt and pepper.

4 Pour the fondue into a fondue pot or a warmed serving dish set on a heated tray or over an appropriate burner. Dip chunks of crusty bread, carrot or apple into the pan on long-handled forks to scoop up the cheese.

....

COOK'S TIP: The courgette and apple in the fondue really mask the richness of the dish, making it ideal for informal entertaining.
If the fondue cools and starts to set, reheat it gently, stirring constantly.

SERVES 6
PREPARATION TIME: 10 minutes
COOKING TIME: about 10 minutes

2 shallots
1 red chilli
1 green chilli
1 courgette, trimmed
1 crisp eating apple, quartered and cored (peel left on)
375 ml/1½ cups dry white wine or hard cider
Juice of half a lemon
600 g Swiss cheese, preferably Emmental and Gruyère mixed
2 Tbsp cornflour
Salt and freshly ground black pepper to taste
Chunks of crusty bread, carrots, apple or other vegetables for dipping

EFFORTLESS DESSERTS

Some people love to make desserts and others don't think twice about buying a fruit tart to finish a meal. We have chosen a selection of our favourite flavours (you'll notice that we love chocolate!) and built a group of recipes around them. Some are quick, others require a certain amount of fiddling, but all are utterly delicious and couldn't be easier to do with a mixer.

LEMONGRASS AND LIME MOUSSE

SERVES 4

PREPARATION TIME: 1½ to 2½
   hours, including chilling
   time

COOKING TIME: about 10
   minutes

2 lemongrass stalks, tough
   outer layers removed
60 ml/¼ cup water
2 eggs, separated
   (see note, page 4)
100 g caster sugar
Grated zest of 1 lime, plus
   more for garnishing
Juice of 1½ limes
280 ml/1¼ cups double cream
11.7-g packet powdered
   gelatine

This mousse has a wonderfully delicate flavour and provides a light, clean finish to a meal.

1 Using a rolling pin, thoroughly crush the lemongrass to release its flavour. Place in a saucepan, cover with water and simmer for 10 minutes. Allow to cool in the pan.

2 Meanwhile, using the wire whip, whisk the egg yolk with the sugar on the fastest speed setting until you have a thick, pale mixture. Add the lime zest, lime juice and cream and briefly whisk again.

3 When cool, remove the lemongrass from the pan and discard. Reheat until almost boiling, then sprinkle the gelatine over the liquid, remove from the heat and stir until the gelatine has dissolved completely. Allow to cool slightly and then with the mixer running at medium speed, slowly pour the gelatine onto the egg mixture until thoroughly combined. Transfer to another bowl and set aside.

4 Wash the whisk and bowl thoroughly before whisking the egg whites until firm. Add to the mixture in the reserved bowl and fold in until just combined.

5 Pour into four individual serving dishes and refrigerate for one to two hours. Sprinkle with lime zest to serve.

BAKED RICOTTA CHEESECAKE SCENTED WITH ORANGE AND CARDAMOM

SERVES 6 TO 8
PREPARATION TIME: 25 minutes
COOKING TIME: 1 hour

FOR THE BASE:
50 g self-raising flour
½ tsp baking powder
50 g butter
50 g caster sugar
1 egg

FOR THE FILLING:
500 g full fat ricotta cheese
275 g caster sugar
140 ml/½ cup double cream
4 eggs, separated
1 medium orange
6 cardamom pods
¼ tsp salt

Orange zest and chopped
**   pistachio nuts for garnishing**

This cheesecake is amazing – a smooth orange cream with the unique texture of ricotta cheese, combined with the occasional hint of cardamom. Yum!

1 Preheat the oven to 160°C/Gas Mark 3. Grease and line the base of a 23-cm springform tin with baking parchment.

2 Make the base. Sieve the flour and baking powder into the mixer bowl, add the butter, sugar and egg, and beat together at medium speed for two to three minutes, or until you can no longer hear the graininess of the sugar scraping against the bowl. The mixture should be light and pale. Spread it evenly over the bottom of the prepared tin.

3 To make the filling, use the flat beater at medium speed to combine the ricotta and sugar until smooth. Then, beat in the cream and four egg yolks a little at a time. Mix thoroughly between each addition. Transfer to another bowl and refrigerate until needed.

4 Quarter the orange and remove any pips. Then, using the Rotary Slicer and Shredder with the fine shredding drum, shred the whole orange and the cardamom pods. Stir into the ricotta mixture and set aside.

5 Using the wire whip and a clean bowl, whisk two egg whites with the salt until they stand in firm peaks. Gently fold the whites into the ricotta mixture. Pour over the base in the prepared tin and level off.

6 Bake in the oven for about one hour or until just set and golden in colour. A skewer inserted into the centre should come out clean. Turn off the heat but leave the cheesecake in the oven with the door slightly ajar for another 30 minutes, then remove from the oven and allow to cool completely. This stage is most important to prevent the cake from sinking in the middle.

7 To serve, carefully release the sides of the tin and transfer to a serving plate. Decorate with orange zest and a scattering of pistachio nuts.

CLASSIC APPLE PIE

You can't beat classic apple pie served either with custard, whipped cream or ice cream! You can count on this recipe for easy entertaining time and again.

....

1 Preheat the oven to 200°C/Gas Mark 6. Grease a deep 23-cm pie dish.

2 Make the pastry. Sieve the flour and salt into the mixer bowl. Add the butter and shortening and combine using the flat beater at slow speed until the mixture resembles breadcrumbs. Add the egg and then the water a spoonful at a time (you may not need it all) until the mixture comes together as a dough. Cover in clingfilm and refrigerate for about 30 minutes.

3 Roll out two-thirds of the pastry to about a 5-mm thickness and line the pie dish with it, being careful to push the pastry into the edges. Roll out the remaining pastry for the lid of the pie and set aside.

4 Peel, core and slice the apples into a large bowl. Add the remaining ingredients and mix well. Pour into the lined pie dish. Moisten the edges with water or milk and cover with the pastry lid, pressing down the edges to seal. Cut two small slits in the top of the pie to allow steam to escape and sprinkle generously with caster sugar. Bake for 10 minutes before lowering the temperature to 180°C/Gas Mark 4 and cooking for another 30 minutes or until it is a rich golden colour. Serve hot or cold.

SERVES 6 TO 8
PREPARATION TIME: 50 minutes
COOKING TIME: 40 minutes

FOR THE PASTRY:
450 g plain flour
Pinch of salt
100 g butter
100 g vegetable shortening
1 egg, beaten
4 to 6 Tbsp cold water

FOR THE FILLING:
900 g cooking apples
Zest and juice of 1 lemon
100 g caster sugar
2 tsp cinnamon
½ tsp freshly grated nutmeg

Caster sugar for topping

BANOFFEE MERINGUE GATEAU

'Banoffee' is the fun way to describe the heavenly combination of toffee and bananas. This dessert is such a success when entertaining. Not only does it taste amazing and wonderfully naughty, it also looks great with its sumptuous layers and impressive height.

1 Preheat the oven to 140°C/Gas Mark 1. Line the base of two ungreased 18-cm baking tins with baking parchment.

2 First, make the meringue. Using the wire whip, whisk the egg whites with the salt until stiff, then with the motor running at slow speed, add the sugar a teaspoonful at a time. Add the remaining meringue ingredients and combine. Divide the mixture between the two tins and level the surface of each one. Bake on the same shelf, just below the centre of the oven, for about 1½ hours. When the meringue is cooked and firm to the touch, lay a tea towel on a wire rack and turn out each meringue. Remove the baking parchment.

3 When the meringue is cool, whisk the cream until it just begins to thicken. Slice the bananas and cover with lemon juice to prevent them from going brown. Then, begin to assemble the gateau. Take one meringue and place it in the centre of a serving plate. Spoon half of the dulce de leche onto the meringue and spread out evenly. Scatter half the banana slices, followed by half the cream and some grated chocolate. Put the other meringue on top and repeat the process with the remaining ingredients. Finish with a generous amount of grated chocolate and refrigerate until needed.

COOK'S TIP: If you are unable to find Dulce de leche (an Argentinean caramel spread) simmer an unopened can of condensed milk in water for about three hours instead. Be very careful when doing this, however. Follow the manufacturer's instructions and never attempt this if the can has a ring-pull device.

SERVES 6 TO 8

PREPARATION TIME: 25 minutes

COOKING TIME: 1½ hours

FOR THE MERINGUE:

4 egg whites

Pinch of salt

150 g caster sugar

1 tsp vanilla extract

1 tsp white wine vinegar

2 level Tbsp cornflour

25 g chopped roasted hazelnuts

FOR THE FILLING

280 ml/1¼ cups double cream

3 large bananas

Juice of half a lemon

450 g/2 cups Dulce de leche (Banoffee Toffee)

50 g good-quality dark chocolate, grated (minimum 70% cocoa solids)

INDIVIDUAL
MARMALADE PUDDINGS

MAKES 6 INDIVIDUAL PUDDINGS
PREPARATION TIME: 15 minutes
COOKING TIME: 20 to 25 minutes

6 Tbsp orange marmalade
125 g self-raising flour
100 g caster sugar
100 g butter, softened

These puddings use the easy, all-in-one cake method to produce delicate individual desserts with no fuss and at very little cost. You will need six small pudding basins or ramekins (about 175-ml capacity each) and six lightly greased 15-cm squares of kitchen foil.

1 Preheat the oven to 180°C/Gas Mark 4. Grease the pudding basins thoroughly and put 1 tablespoon of marmalade into the bottom of each one.
2 Sieve the flour into the mixer bowl and add all the other ingredients. Combine using the flat beater until well mixed and smooth.

3 Spoon the mixture equally into the prepared basins and level the surface of each one. Cover each basin with a square of greased foil and place on a baking tray. Bake for about 20 to 25 minutes or until the sponge bounces back when pressed lightly.

4 Loosen the edges of each pudding with a knife and then turn out onto individual dessert plates. Serve immediately with softly whipped cream.

COOK'S TIP: When serving, try flavouring the softly whipped cream with Drambuie or Cointreau and a little sieved icing sugar to taste.

2 eggs, beaten
I tsp ground ginger
Softly whipped cream for serving

LEMON IMPOSSIBLE PUDDING

Far from being "impossible" to make, this pudding is so named because it seems impossible that the unusual looking batter could come out of the oven as a light sponge floating on a delicious puddle of lemon sauce. This recipe has been a family favourite for years.

SERVES 4
PREPARATION TIME: 20 minutes
COOKING TIME: 50 minutes

3 eggs, separated
75 g caster sugar
200 ml/¾ cup milk
I Tbsp self-raising flour, sieved
Grated zest and juice of 2 large lemons
Pinch of salt
Hot water (see method)

I Preheat the oven to 180°C/Gas Mark 4. Grease a deep ovenproof dish (about I litre capacity). Stand this in a roasting tin.

2 Using the wire whip, mix the egg yolks with the sugar until light and creamy, then add the milk, flour, lemon zest and lemon juice and whisk until well combined. The mixture will probably separate and look as if something has gone horribly wrong! But don't worry, simply transfer to a separate bowl and set aside.

3 Thoroughly wash and dry the mixing bowl before whisking the whites and salt together until stiff. Fold into the lemon mixture with a metal spoon.

4 Transfer the mixture to the prepared dish and then pour hot water into the roasting tray to come half way up the side of the dish. Bake for about 50 minutes or until risen and lightly golden. Serve immediately.

BAILEYS CHOCOLATE TART

This decadent dessert is always a showstopper, whether entertaining formally or at a relaxed lunch, morning coffee or afternoon tea! This is for serious chocoholics and Baileys fans only!

....

1 Make the pastry. Sieve the flour, icing sugar, cocoa and salt into the mixer bowl and combine with the butter using the flat beater at the slowest speed until the mixture resembles breadcrumbs. Add the yolk and mix until it begins to come together. Gather the dough into a ball with your hands and cover with clingfilm. Refrigerate for 30 minutes.

2 Preheat the oven to 170°C/Gas Mark 3. Grease a 23-cm flan tin that has a removable bottom. On a lightly floured surface, roll the pastry out to about a 6-mm thickness. Lay the pastry in the tin and press firmly into the edges. Carefully line the pastry with kitchen foil or baking parchment. Weigh the tart down with pie weights, dried beans, or rice and bake for 30 minutes. Remove the tart from the oven, remove the beans and foil or paper and allow to cool in the tin on a wire rack.

3 While the pastry case is cooling, make the filling. Whisk the double cream until it just begins to thicken. Melt the milk chocolate by placing it in the microwave in a microwave-safe bowl on high power for 1½ minutes. Remove and stir to dissolve any lumps. Add the Baileys to the melted chocolate and stir thoroughly. The mixture will become very thick, but don't worry; simply add a spoon of the whipped cream and mix together. Continue this process until you have about 2 tablespoons of whipped cream remaining. Fold the remaining cream into the chocolate, but this time, do not combine thoroughly so you are left with a marbled effect.

4 When the pastry is cool, melt the dark chocolate and use a pastry brush to "paint" the inside of the pastry case with it. Allow this chocolate to set, about two to five minutes, and then pour the filling into the pastry case and smooth the surface. Refrigerate for at least one hour or until needed. Serve dusted with cocoa powder and accompanied by fruit, such as sliced oranges or raspberries (to help cut through the richness of the dessert).

SERVES 6 TO 8

PREPARATION TIME: 1 hour and 45 minutes, including chilling time

COOKING TIME: 30 minutes

FOR THE PASTRY:

125 g plain flour

50 g icing sugar

1 Tbsp cocoa powder, plus extra for dusting

½ tsp salt

100 g butter, chilled and diced

1 egg yolk

FOR THE FILLING:

280 ml/1¼ cups double cream

200 g luxury milk chocolate

2 Tbsp Baileys Original Irish Cream® or other Irish cream liqueur (or to taste!)

30 g luxury dark chocolate (minimum 70% cocoa solids)

BAKED FIG AND MASCARPONE TART WITH WALNUT PRALINE

SERVES 6 TO 8

PREPARATION TIME: 40
    minutes, plus 2 to 12 hours
    for chilling

COOKING TIME: 1 hour

FOR THE PÂTE SUCRÉE:
200 g plain flour, sieved
1 level Tbsp caster sugar
Pinch of salt
100 g butter, chilled and diced
1 egg, beaten

FOR THE PRALINE:
100 g caster sugar
60 ml/¼ cup water
75 g walnut pieces

FOR THE FILLING:
5 dried figs, sliced
400 g mascarpone cheese
50 g unsalted butter, softened
50 g caster sugar
3 eggs
1 tsp grated lemon zest

Softly whipped cream for
    serving

This fantastic dessert will keep guests coming back for more! It combines a crisp pâte sucrée base (traditional French sweet pastry), soft mascarpone custard with dried figs and a seriously crunchy walnut praline topping. There's a lot going on, but the flavours and textures marry perfectly.

1 Make the pastry. Sieve the flour, sugar and salt into the mixer bowl and combine using the flat beater. Then add the butter and mix on a slow speed until the mixture resembles breadcrumbs. Add the egg and continue mixing until the dough comes together. Cover it in clingfilm and refrigerate for 30 minutes.

2 Meanwhile, make the walnut praline. Grease a baking tray (that has sides) and set aside. In a small pan over low heat, combine the sugar with the water until the sugar dissolves. Increase the heat and boil the syrup without stirring until it becomes a light caramel colour. This will take about three to five minutes. Add the nuts and stir gently to coat evenly, then spoon onto the prepared baking tray and make level with the back of the spoon. Set aside to cool completely, by which time the mixture will have solidified. Using a knife, shatter or roughly chop the praline into about 1-cm shards.

3 Preheat the oven to 180°C/Gas Mark 4. Grease a 23-cm flan tin that has a removable bottom. Remove the pastry from the refrigerator and roll out on a lightly floured surface to about a 6-mm thickness. Line the prepared tin with the pastry, pinching the edges with thumb and forefinger to make it look more attractive. Line with kitchen foil or baking parchment and weigh down with pie weights, dried beans or rice. Bake for 10 minutes, then remove the weights and the foil or paper and bake for another 10 minutes. Remove from the oven and allow to cool in the tin on a wire rack. Reduce the oven temperature to 170°C/Gas Mark 3.

4 While the pastry is baking, make the filling. Combine the mascarpone cheese, butter and sugar using the flat beater. When the mixture is smooth, add the eggs and lemon zest and mix again. Set aside in a cool place.

5 When the pastry is cool, scatter the sliced figs over the base and pour the mascarpone mixture over the top. Bake for 40 minutes, or until the custard has set. Remove from the oven and immediately sprinkle with the walnut praline and allow to cool in the tin for at least two hours, but preferably about 12 hours. Remove from the tin, slice and serve with lightly whipped cream.

CHOCOLATE AND ALMOND TORTE

This flourless torte is surprisingly light. Use a really good quality chocolate with at least 70% cocoa solids for a slightly bitter, light result. Serve with whipped cream or soured cream – or a toffee ice cream – and decorate with chocolate curls or soft seasonal fruits.

SERVES 8 TO 10

PREPARATION TIME: 25 to 30 minutes

COOKING TIME: 40 minutes

100 g unsalted butter

150 g good-quality dark chocolate, broken into small pieces

5 eggs, separated

150 g ground almonds

100 g light brown sugar, or light **Muscavado** sugar if available

Icing sugar for dusting

1 Preheat the oven to 160°C/Gas Mark 3. Butter and line the base of a 23-cm springform tin with baking parchment.

2 Melt the butter and chocolate in a large bowl over a pan of hot water, or heat in the microwave for two to three minutes. Cool slightly.

3 Whisk the egg whites, gradually increasing the speed, until they form stiff peaks. Meanwhile, add the egg yolks, almonds and brown sugar to the chocolate and mix well.

4 Lightly and gently fold the egg whites into the chocolate in three batches with a large metal spoon. Scrape the mixture into the prepared tin, gently tapping the sides to level the top, and bake for 35 to 40 minutes until set. Allow the torte to cool in the tin.

5 Dust with icing sugar before slicing and serving.

COOK'S TIP: Always add the egg whites to the chocolate mixture, and not the other way around, or the resulting torte will be heavy.

COFFEE CREAM ECLAIRS

MAKES ABOUT 12 ECLAIRS
PREPARATION TIME: 20 minutes
COOKING TIME: 30 minutes

FOR THE PASTY:
250 ml/1 cup water
50 g butter
125 g plain flour (sieved into
   a square of baking
   parchment)
Pinch of salt
1 egg yolk, beaten
2 whole eggs, beaten

FOR THE ICING:
125 g icing sugar
1 Tbsp instant coffee granules
1 Tbsp hot water

FOR THE FILLING:
280 ml/1¼ cups double cream
1 Tbsp Tía Maria (optional)

It seems everybody loves cream éclairs! These are topped with coffee icing and we give you the option of making a Tía Maria cream filling. Your mixer takes all the effort out of making choux pastry and produces fabulous results.

1 Preheat the oven to 220°C/Gas Mark 7 and lightly grease a baking tray.

2 Make the choux pastry. Melt the butter in the water in a saucepan over a low heat, then bring to a rapid boil. Add the flour and beat quickly with a wooden spoon until mixed, then pour into the mixer bowl and beat on a medium speed for one minute, or until the mixture leaves the sides of the bowl cleanly. Allow to cool for a few minutes. Gradually add the beaten egg, mixing slowly at first and then a little faster. The mixture should hold its shape, so only add as much of the egg as is necessary.

3 Fill an icing bag fitted with a 2-cm plain tip with the pastry mixture and pipe twelve 10-cm lengths onto the prepared baking tray. Bake for 10 minutes, then lower the oven temperature to 180°C/Gas Mark 4 and bake for another 15 minutes or until risen and golden. Remove from the oven and immediately cut along the length of each éclair to let the steam escape. There should not be any moist dough remaining in the centre of the éclairs. If there is, return them to the oven (which has been switched off) for about two minutes, by which time they should be cooked through. Allow to cool completely on a wire rack.

4 While the éclairs are cooling, make the icing by combining the ingredients and mixing thoroughly. Allow to stand until needed.

5 For the filling, whisk the double cream until firm, then add the Tía Maria if you are using it. Whisk again to combine. When the pastry is cool, fill an icing bag (fitted with the same size tip as before) with the whipped cream and neatly fill each éclair. Top each one with about 1 to 2 teaspoons of icing and put aside to set before serving.

PUMPKIN PIE

Pumpkin pie is a classic, but here it is given a slight twist with the addition of soured cream to the filling and ground ginger to the pastry base.

1 Grease a 23-cm loose bottomed fluted flan tin.

2 Make the pastry. Sieve the flour, salt and ginger into the mixer bowl. Add the butter and using the flat beater at slow speed, combine until the mixture resembles breadcrumbs. Add enough cold water, a spoonful at a time, to make a firm dough. Bring the dough together with your hands, and on a lightly floured surface, roll out to about a 6-mm thickness. Line the prepared tin with the pastry, pinching the edges with thumb and forefinger to make it look more attractive. Refrigerate for 30 minutes.

3 Meanwhile, make the filling. Preheat the oven to 200°C/Gas Mark 6. Using the flat beater, purée the cooked pumpkin, then add the brown sugar, salt and spices and mix again before adding the remaining ingredients and combining thoroughly. The filling should be smooth and runny in consistency.

4 Pour the filling into the chilled pastry case and bake for 15 minutes before lowering the temperature to 180°C/Gas Mark 4. Cook for another 45 minutes or until just set; the tip of a knife inserted into the centre of the pie should come out clean. Cool the pie for at least an hour before serving with whipped cream or ice cream.

COOK'S TIP: For this recipe, we use a pumpkin weighing about 450 g. Peel it, remove the seeds and cut it into rough cubes. Place it in a bowl with 2 tablespoons of water, cover and cook in the microwave for about 10 minutes, or until soft. Alternatively, you can steam the peeled and seeded pumpkin in a covered steamer over a pan of boiling water.

SERVES 6 TO 8
PREPARATION TIME: 40 minutes
COOKING TIME: 60 minutes

FOR THE PASTRY:
200 g plain flour
½ tsp salt
1 tsp ground ginger
100 g butter, chilled and diced
3 to 4 Tbsp cold water

FOR THE FILLING:
500 ml/2 cups cooked pumpkin (see Cook's tip below)
150 g soft light brown sugar
Pinch of salt
2 tsp cinnamon
½ tsp freshly grated nutmeg
3 eggs, beaten
125 ml/½ cup creme fraiche
125 ml/½ cup milk

CRANACHAN CREAM

This traditional Scottish dessert looks and tastes great. An added advantage with this recipe is that it can be made quickly and easily and then left in the refrigerator for up to six hours before being served.

....

1 Place the oatmeal in a baking tin and toast under a preheated grill for three to five minutes, or until golden. Shake the tin frequently to ensure that the oatmeal browns evenly. Remove from the tin and set aside.

2 Whip the cream with the wire whip just until it begins to thicken, then add the sugar and whisky and briefly whisk to combine.

3 Using four 250-ml glasses (or one large glass serving dish) begin layering the ingredients by putting a spoonful of cream into each one. Follow this with a few raspberries and a scattering of oatmeal. Continue this process to create haphazard layers, which look (and possibly taste) better. Finish with a dusting of oatmeal and garnish with three perfect raspberries per serving. Refrigerate until needed.

....

COOK'S TIP: Don't be tempted to whip the cream too much, because the texture of the dessert will become dry.

SERVES 4

PREPARATION TIME: 20 minutes

COOKING TIME: 3 to 5 minutes

100 g oatmeal

280 ml/1¼ cups double cream

1 heaped Tbsp caster sugar

1 to 2 Tbsp whisky (to taste)

150 g fresh raspberries, hulled, with extra for garnishing

GRAPEFRUIT SORBET WITH VERMOUTH

SERVES 6 TO 8

PREPARATION TIME: about 1 hour and 20 minutes, including cooling and chilling time

FREEZING TIME: 3 to 4 hours without an ice cream machine, 30 minutes with

3 grapefruits, grated and juiced

2 cinnamon sticks

200 g caster sugar

2 egg whites (see note, page 4)

Vermouth to serve (extra dry, or to taste)

Sorbet is really refreshing at the end of a meal and this is one of the best recipes that we have come across. Creamy-white in colour, it needs just a generous splash of vermouth poured over it before serving.

....

1 Measure the grapefruit juice and bring it up to 750 ml/3 cups with as much water as is necessary. Place in a pan with the grated rind and cinnamon sticks and bring to the boil. Cover and leave for five minutes, then discard the cinnamon sticks. Stir in the sugar to dissolve, then strain the mixture into a bowl. Allow to cool, then chill for one hour.

2 Whisk the egg whites in the mixer bowl until white and fluffy but not stiff. Pour in the chilled grapefruit mixture and continue whisking until well combined. Pour into an ice cream maker and freeze-churn until ready to serve. Alternatively, pour into a suitable plastic container and freeze for three to four hours, stirring vigorously at least twice.

3 Serve in scoops with a good splash of vermouth.

....

COOK'S TIP: Allow the sorbet to stand in the refrigerator for 20 to 30 minutes or so before serving if it has been frozen solid. If it is melting unevenly, pour into the mixer bowl and mix with the flat beater to make it smooth. Serve immediately, or freeze again until scoopable.

RHUBARB AND ORANGE PAVLOVA

Of course you can use any fruit you like on a Pavlova, but rhubarb and orange is unusual and very good! Your mixer makes the perfect meringue – just remember to add the sugar slowly, a small spoonful at a time.

SERVES 6 TO 8

PREPARATION TIME: 30 minutes

COOKING TIME: 2 to 2 ½ hours

4 egg whites
  (see note, page 4)
Pinch of salt
200 g caster sugar, plus some for sprinkling
½ tsp cream of tartar
1 Tbsp cornflour
½ tsp vanilla extract
1 tsp white wine vinegar
350 g cleaned rhubarb
4 Tbsp water
4 Tbsp sugar
2 oranges
280 ml/1 ¼ cups double cream

1 Preheat the oven to 160°C/Gas Mark 3. Line a baking tray with baking parchment, draw a 25-cm circle on the paper and sprinkle with a little caster sugar.

2 Whisk the egg whites with the salt until stiff. Start slowly and gradually increase the speed of your mixer.

3 With the motor still running, whisk in the sugar, a small spoonful at a time. This will not take as long as you think and it is well worth the extra time to incorporate the sugar slowly. Mix the cream of tartar and the cornflour in with the last of the sugar and add to the egg whites, then add the vanilla extract and vinegar. The resulting meringue should be stiff, thick and glossy.

4 Pile the meringue onto the prepared baking tray and spread it out to cover the marked circle. Bake for two hours, or two and a half hours if you like your meringue crisp through to the middle. Allow to cool.

5 Cut the rhubarb into 5-cm lengths and place in a pan with the water and sugar. Cover and cook slowly for 10 minutes, until just tender. Grate the zest from the oranges into the pan, then roughly chop the flesh, mix into the pan and then remove from the heat. Allow to cool.

6 Place the meringue on a serving platter. Whisk the double cream until it forms soft peaks and pile onto the centre of the cooked meringue. Top with the rhubarb and orange mixture, and spoon some of the juices over each serving.

MANGO MERINGUE ROULADE

SERVES 8 TO 10
PREPARATION TIME: 30 minutes
  plus chilling time
COOKING TIME: 20 to 25
  minutes

5 egg whites (save the yolks to
  make your own fruit curd)
  (see note, page 4)
300 g caster sugar
50 g desiccated coconut
280 ml/1¼ cups double cream
1 large ripe mango, peeled
  and diced
Passion fruit, raspberries or
  physallis to decorate

A meringue roulade is a light but indulgent dessert and perfect any time of year with whatever fruits are in season. It's also delicious filled with whipped cream mixed with citrus curd or cheese – orange, lemon, or lime all work well. This freezes admirably.

1 Preheat the oven to 190°C/Gas Mark 5. Line a Swiss-roll tin (about 30 × 22 cm) with baking parchment.

2 Whisk the egg whites until very stiff, starting slowly and then gradually increasing the mixer speed. Keep whisking on a high speed and add the sugar a spoonful at a time. Whisk well between each addition; the meringue will be very stiff and firm when finished. Pile it into the prepared tin and spread evenly, scattering the coconut over the smoothed surface.

3 Bake for 20 to 25 minutes, until lightly browned and firm to the touch. The meringue may have cracked a bit, but it doesn't matter.

4 Transfer the meringue to a wire rack lined with more baking parchment. Any darkly browned coconut will hopefully fall off at this stage! Remove the baked paper and allow to cool for 10 to 15 minutes.

5 Whisk the cream to form soft peaks, gradually increasing the mixer speed. Fold in the mango and any mango juice with a spoon and then spread the cream evenly over the meringue. Make a deep incision along one of the long sides and then roll up, using the baking parchment to help. Be sure to roll firmly and tightly so the roulade will keep its shape. Chill, wrapped in the paper, for at least an hour or two before serving.

6 To serve, remove the paper and cut into slices. Arrange on a platter and decorate with seasonal fruits; passion fruit is especially delicious drizzled over each slice.

COOK'S TIP: For a slightly crisper meringue, bake at 220°C/Gas Mark 7 for 10 to 12 minutes, or until browned and slightly firm, then reduce the heat to 160°C/Gas Mark 3 and cook for another 15 to 20 minutes until "solid".

CAKES AND BAKES

This is traditionally where a mixer really comes into its own! Everyone loves a home-made cake, and we have a selection of traditional and contemporary bakes for every occasion. Your mixer will cream and whisk to perfection, but remember to check out the blueprint recipes and mixing tips at the beginning of the book before you start, especially if you are a novice baker.

TROPICAL FRUIT CAKE

MAKES 1 LARGE CAKE

PREPARATION TIME: 30
minutes, plus overnight
soaking

COOKING TIME: 2 to 2 ¼ hours

250 g sultanas
150 g raisins
100 g currants
275-ml bottle Bacardi
Breezer® (orange,
pineapple or watermelon)
250 g dried mixed tropical
fruits
100 g glacé cherries
100 g desiccated coconut
100 g macadamia nuts,
roughly chopped
150 g marzipan, cut into 1-cm
chunks
125 g plain flour
½ tsp ground mace
½ tsp baking powder
Pinch of salt
50 g butter, at room
temperature
100 g caster sugar
75 g light brown sugar, or light
Muscovado sugar if available
2 eggs
½ tsp almond extract

This is a fabulously exotic cake, loaded with tropical fruit, coconut and more than a touch of alcohol. It's special enough to cover with icing for a special occasion, and it's sophisticated enough to nibble, just as it is, with a cocktail by the pool.

1 Soak the sultanas, raisins and currants in half the Bacardi Breezer, cover and leave overnight. Don't drink the rest of the Bacardi – you'll certainly need some of it for the recipe!

2 Snip the tropical fruits into roughly 1-cm chunks and cut the cherries in half. Add to the soaked fruits along with the coconut and macadamia nuts and mix well. Add the marzipan.

3 Preheat the oven to 170°C/Gas Mark 3. Oil a 23-cm round cake tin and line the base with baking parchment.

4 Sieve together the flour, mace, baking powder and salt.

5 Combine the butter and sugars in the mixing bowl with the flat beater on a low speed; there's too much sugar for the mixture to become creamy, but it will blend together. Add the eggs one at a time, slightly increasing the speed to achieve a more traditional cake-like batter, then add the almond extract and the sieved flour mixture. Beat thoroughly for one minute.

6 Add the soaked fruits and nuts, with any remaining liquid, mixing slowly to combine all the ingredients. Pile the mixture into the prepared tin, pressing down firmly; the tin will be full, but the cake hardly rises during baking.

7 Bake for about two hours, or until a dark golden colour. If the cake is browning too quickly, cover with kitchen foil or baking parchment. Test with a skewer inserted into the centre of the cake; if it comes out clean and the fruit is no longer "singing", the cake is done. When testing for doneness, try to avoid the chunks of marzipan because it will make the skewer come out sticky.

8 Leave the cake to cool in the tin. When cold, remove it carefully and make lots of holes in the top and bottom with a skewer. Spoon some of the remaining Bacardi over the surface, allowing it to soak in. Don't make it too moist!

9 Wrap in foil and leave to mature for at least a couple of days – a couple of weeks is best. Serve in generous slices, as the large pieces of fruit and nut will cause the cake to crumble.

PUMPKIN, RUM AND RAISIN CAKE

Add a little whipped cream to a piece of the cake and serve with coffee.

....

1 Soak the raisins in the rum for at least 10 minutes, the longer the better.

2 Preheat the oven to 180°C/Gas Mark 4 and line the base of a large loaf tin with baking parchment.

3 If using freshly cooked pumpkin or squash, cut into chunks and place in the mixer bowl. Beat until smooth on a medium speed using the flat beater.

4 If using canned pumpkin, add it now. Add the margarine, brown sugar, eggs and self-raising flour and beat together on a medium speed until thoroughly blended. Add the raisins and the rum and continue mixing for another minute.

5 Pour into the prepared tin and bake for one hour. Cool slightly in the tin, then turn out onto a wire rack to cool completely.

MAKES I LARGE CAKE
PREPARATION TIME: 30 minutes, or I ½ hours if roasting pumpkin
COOKING TIME: I hour

150 g raisins
50 ml/¼ cup dark rum
Half a 400-g can pumpkin purée, or 200 g cooked pumpkin or squash
150 g soft margarine
150 g light brown sugar, or light Muscovado sugar if available
2 eggs
250 g self-raising flour

DATE AND OAT SLICE

This has long been a favourite treat – rich, filling, and ever so easy to make.

....

1 Preheat oven to 180°C/Gas Mark 4. Lightly butter a 20-cm round cake tin.

2 Cook the dates and water together gently in a tin until the dates are soft and the water slightly reduced.

3 Meanwhile, pour the melted butter into the mixer bowl, add the flour, brown sugar and oats and mix well using the flat beater. Press half the mixture into the prepared tin, and transfer the rest to a plate and set aside.

4 Pour the dates and water into the mixer bowl, add the vanilla extract and beat until smooth. Spread the dates over the batter in the tin, then top with the remaining oat mixture.

5 Bake for 30 minutes, until lightly browned and set. Mark into slices in the tin while still warm and leave in the tin to cool. Cut into slices when almost cold. Store in an airtight container.

SERVES 8
PREPARATION TIME: 20 minutes
COOKING TIME: 30 minutes

250 g dried dates, roughly chopped
150 ml/⅔ cup water
150 g butter, melted
125 g plain flour
150 g light brown sugar, or light Muscovado sugar if available
150 g rolled oats
I tsp vanilla extract

CRANBERRY AND ORANGE CRUMBLE CAKE

MAKES 1 LARGE CAKE

PREPARATION TIME: 30 minutes

COOKING TIME: about 1½ hours

200 g fresh, or frozen defrosted cranberries

2 oranges, peeled and roughly chopped

FOR THE TOPPING:

100 g self-raising wholemeal flour (or 100 g plain wholemeal flour and 2 tsp baking powder)

100 g butter

100 g Demerara sugar

FOR THE CAKE:

150 g butter

150 g light brown sugar, or light Muscovado sugar if available

3 eggs, beaten

250 g self-raising flour

1 tsp ground cinnamon

Crumble cakes are a delicious half-way point between a pudding and a cake. They are lovely warm with custard or cream and wonderful when cold. This is an excellent cake to serve with morning coffee.

1 Preheat the oven to 180°C/Gas Mark 4. Line a 23-cm springform tin with baking parchment.

2 Mix together the cranberries and oranges and set aside.

3 Prepare the topping. Blend the wholemeal flour and butter on a medium speed with the flat beater until the mixture resembles lumpy breadcrumbs, then mix in the sugar. Transfer the topping to a plate.

4 Make the cake. Cream the butter and brown sugar together with the flat beater until pale in colour. Gradually add the eggs, beating well after each addition; the mixture may start to curdle but keep beating. Fold in the self-raising flour and cinnamon on the lowest speed until blended. The mixture should be quite stiff.

5 Carefully spoon the cake mixture into the bottom of the prepared tin and scatter first the fruits and then the topping, over the cake.

6 Bake for about one and a half hours, until a skewer inserted into the cake comes out clean. For a pudding-like cake, allow to cool slightly in the tin and serve warm. For a traditional cake, remove from the tin to a wire rack and allow to cool completely before serving.

COOK'S TIP: Make the cake with cranberry and orange sauce when fresh fruit is not available. However, store the finished cake in the refrigerator if made with fresh fruits.

TRADITIONAL CARROT CAKE WITH CREAM CHEESE FROSTING

MAKES 1 LARGE CAKE
PREPARATION TIME: 20 minutes
COOKING TIME: 1 hour

FOR THE CARROT CAKE:
175 g caster sugar
185 ml/¾ cup sunflower or
    vegetable oil
2 eggs, beaten
175 g self-raising flour, sieved
1 tsp pumpkin spice
½ tsp salt
½ Tbsp honey
200 g carrots, coarsely grated
    using the Slicer & Shredder
    attachment
25 g walnut pieces, plus more
    for garnishing
25 g raisins

FOR CREAM CHEESE FROSTING:
80 g cream cheese
25 g butter, at room
    temperature
1 Tbsp lemon juice
1 tsp lemon zest
100 g icing sugar

We love this recipe, as it is consistently good and so easy to make! If you prefer a round cake, use a 20-cm round cake tin.

1 Preheat the oven to 170°C/Gas Mark 3. Oil and line the base of a large loaf tin with baking parchment.

2 Make the cake. Combine the sugar, oil and eggs in the mixer bowl and beat until thick and pale, using the flat beater on a medium high setting. Add the flour, spice, salt and honey, and continue to beat until blended.

3 Stir in the remaining cake ingredients, then pour the mixture into the prepared tin and bake for one hour or until a skewer inserted into the cake comes out clean. Allow to cool in the tin for about five minutes and then turn out onto a wire rack to cool completely.

4 Make the frosting. Beat the cream cheese, butter, lemon juice and zest together using the flat beater, then beat in the icing sugar. Spread the frosting on top of the cooled cake and decorate with walnut pieces.

COOK'S TIP: You simply cannot make frosting with low-fat cream cheese; it becomes very runny and will not coat the cake. Full fat cheese is the only way!

ANGEL CAKE WITH ORANGE GLAZE

The orange glaze makes this light cake look incredibly attractive. Sieving the flour four times sounds excessive, but it is necessary in order for the cake to be a success.

....

1 Preheat the oven 190°C/Gas Mark 3. Grease a 25-cm ring mould.

2 Sieve the flour four times and set aside. Whisk the egg whites with the salt and cream of tartar until soft peaks form. With the motor still running, gradually whisk the sugar into the egg whites, a teaspoon at a time. Take the time to do this slowly.

3 Fold the flour into the egg whites in three batches using a metal spoon. Work quickly and lightly. Then, add the vanilla extract. Pour into the prepared ring mould and bake for 35 to 40 minutes or until very lightly golden in colour. Allow to cool in the mould upside down on a wire rack.

4 When completely cool, loosen the edges of the cake with a sharp knife and then turn the cake out onto a serving plate, tapping the mould to release it.

5 To make the glaze, simply combine the ingredients and mix well until smooth. Let stand for five minutes and then pour over the top of the cake and leave in a cool place to set.

....

COOK'S TIP: The sieving of the flour and the cooling of the cake upside down in the mould are essential stages in making a successful Angel Cake.

MAKES 1 LARGE CAKE
PREPARATION TIME: 15 minutes
COOKING TIME: 35 to 40 minutes

FOR THE CAKE:
100 g plain flour
6 egg whites
¼ tsp salt
½ tsp cream of tartar
200 g caster sugar
2 tsp vanilla extract

FOR THE GLAZE:
Grated rind of 1 orange
2 Tbsp orange juice
60 g icing sugar, sieved

SPONGE SANDWICH CAKE WITH YOGHURT AND RASPBERRY FILLING

This is the most traditional of cakes and yields a wonderfully moist and springy sponge sandwich. Usually filled with jam and topped with a sprinkling of sugar, here we combine yoghurt and raspberries for a fabulous treat.

MAKES I LARGE CAKE
PREPARATION TIME: 20 minutes
COOKING TIME: 20 to 25 minutes

125 g butter
125 g caster sugar
2 eggs, lightly beaten
125 g self-raising flour, sieved
½ tsp baking powder
About 250 ml/I cup unsweetened yoghurt
150 g fresh raspberries

I Preheat the oven to 180°C/Gas Mark 4. Lightly grease and line the base of two 18-cm round sandwich tins with baking parchment.

2 Using the flat beater, beat together the butter and the sugar until pale and fluffy and you are certain that all the sugar has been dissolved. Add half the eggs to the mixture and beat again until well combined, then beat in the remaining eggs (adding a tablespoon of flour if the mixture looks as if it might curdle).

3 Add the sieved flour and baking powder to the bowl and fold in on the slowest setting until just combined. The batter should be soft and flick easily off a spoon. If necessary, fold in up to 2 tablespoons water (or raspberry liqueur if you are feeling frivolous!) to achieve this consistency.

4 Spoon into the prepared tins and bake on the same shelf in the oven to ensure even cooking, for about 20 to 25 minutes or until the sponge springs back when pressed lightly.

5 Cool for five minutes in the tins, then turn out onto a wire rack to cool completely.

6 Fold the raspberries into the yoghurt and use as a filling between the two cakes, sandwiching them together.

COOK'S TIP: If you wish, you could put more of the yoghurt mixture on top of the cake, too, and then decorate with more raspberries and mint leaves.

WHITE CHOCOLATE TRUFFLE CAKE

MAKES I LARGE CAKE
PREPARATION TIME: 60
 minutes, including chilling
 time for topping
COOKING TIME: 40 minutes

FOR THE CAKE:
150 g unsalted butter,
 softened
300 g caster sugar
4 eggs, beaten
I tsp vanilla extract
325 g plain flour
2 ½ tsp baking powder
½ tsp salt
280 ml/I ¼ cups milk
250 g white chocolate, melted

FOR THE TRUFFLE TOPPING:
250 g white chocolate
280 ml/I ¼ cups double cream
2 egg whites
 (see note, page 4)
White or dark chocolate
 shavings for decoration
 (see method)

Chocolate heaven – this cake not only tastes fabulous but looks really stunning, too. The cake is improved if, after cooling, you wrap it in clingfilm and store overnight before topping with the truffle mixture and then serving.

1 Preheat the oven to 180°C/Gas Mark 4. Grease and line the base of two round 18-cm cake tins with baking parchment.

2 Beat the butter at a low speed with the flat beater to soften. Add the sugar and beat until fluffy, then add the eggs, one at a time, beating well between each addition. Add the vanilla extract. Sieve the dry ingredients into the bowl in three separate stages, beating in at a low speed and adding the milk. Add the melted chocolate and mix well.

3 Divide the batter between the two tins, smooth the tops and bake for 40 minutes or until a skewer inserted into the middle of each cake comes out clean. Cool in the tins for 10 minutes and then turn out onto a wire rack to cool completely.

4 To make the topping, melt the chocolate and allow to cool slightly before adding the cream and stirring thoroughly. Using the wire whip, whisk the whites in the mixer until firm peaks form and then fold the egg whites into the chocolate mixture. Spread half the mixture onto one of the cakes, then top with the other cake and spread the remaining mixture over the top and sides of the cake. Complete with white and/or dark chocolate shavings that can be made using the fine shredding drum of the Rotary Slicer and Shredder. Chill for at least half an hour before serving.

SERIOUSLY LEMONY LEMON BARS

This fabulous recipe uses the all-in-one cake method, so it's very quick and easy to make. The things to remember are that the butter must be very soft and that extra baking powder is needed because air is not beaten into the mixture during an initial creaming process. As a dessert, it is better eaten after about 12 hours and will keep well for several days in a cool place. It also freezes well.

....

1 Preheat the oven to 180°C/Gas Mark 4. Grease a rectangular baking tin (32 x 23 x 4 cm).

2 Make the pastry base. Combine the flour and salt in the mixer bowl and then blend in the butter using the flat beater on a slow speed until the mixture resembles fine breadcrumbs. Add the sugar and eggs gradually to form a dough.

3 Transfer the pastry to a floured surface and roll out to fit the prepared tin, pressing the pastry against the edges of the tin. Chill in the refrigerator while you continue with the recipe.

4 Make the lemon sponge cake. Put all the cake ingredients except for the zest, juice and lemon curd into the mixer bowl and combine on a medium speed. Add the zest and juice and mix in quickly.

5 Spread the lemon curd evenly over the chilled pastry, then spread the cake mixture over and smooth the top.

6 Bake for about 40 minutes until risen and golden brown. The sponge should spring back when pressed gently. Leave in the tin to cool, preferably overnight, and then cut into fingers.

MAKES ABOUT 25 LARGE SLICES
PREPARATION TIME: 35 minutes
COOKING TIME: 40 minutes

FOR SWEET PASTRY BASE:
200 g plain flour, sieved
Pinch of salt
150 g butter, chilled and cut into cubes
1 Tbsp caster sugar
2 eggs, beaten

FOR LEMON SPONGE CAKE:
250 g self-raising flour, sieved
1 tsp baking powder
200 g caster sugar
200 g butter, very soft
4 eggs, beaten
Grated zest of 1 lemon
2 Tbsp lemon juice
225 g lemon curd

CHOCA-MOCHA COLA CAKE

MAKES I LARGE CAKE
PREPARATION TIME: **20 minutes**
COOKING TIME: **40 minutes**

FOR THE CAKE:
225 g self-raising flour
200 g caster sugar
¼ tsp baking soda
200 g butter
50 g cocoa powder
200 ml/¾ cup cola
2 Tbsp instant coffee granules
100 ml/½ cup milk
I egg, beaten
I tsp vanilla extract

FOR THE TOPPING:
50 g cocoa powder, sieved
I Tbsp golden syrup
25 g butter
100 ml/½ cup cola
I Tbsp instant coffee granules

It is difficult to imagine this cake without tasting it first, but it is a wonderfully moist, rich chocolate sponge with an incredible topping. It is great served slightly warm with ice cream!

I Preheat the oven to 180°C/Gas Mark 4. Grease a 25-cm springform tin.

2 Make the cake. In the mixer bowl, combine the flour, sugar and baking soda using the flat beater. Melt the butter with the cocoa, cola and coffee granules in a small saucepan over low heat. Allow to cool slightly, then drizzle the cocoa mixture into the dry ingredients with the mixer running on a slow speed and mix until combined.

3 Add the milk, egg and vanilla extract and mix thoroughly. Pour into the prepared tin and bake for 40 minutes. Allow to cool in the tin for 15 minutes before turning out onto a wire rack.

4 To make the topping, simply combine the ingredients in a saucepan and melt over medium heat, beating the mixture to remove any lumps. Bring to the boil and simmer for 5 minutes. Allow to cool and then spread evenly over the cake. Serve immediately or leave in a cool place until ready to serve.

BANANA AND
SUNFLOWER BREAD

This tea bread is a great way of using up over-ripe bananas. It is best eaten when lightly spread with butter and honey. If covered, it will keep well for several days. It also freezes wonderfully.

1 Preheat the oven to 180°C/Gas Mark 4. Grease and line the base of a large loaf tin with baking parchment.

2 Break the bananas into rough chunks in the mixer bowl and beat them into a purée using the flat beater at a medium speed. Add the eggs, vanilla extract and butter and beat again until well mixed.

3 Add flour, baking powder, salt, spice, sugar and seeds to the bowl and mix well.

4 Pour the mixture into the prepared tin and sprinkle with the reserved seeds. Bake for one hour and 15 minutes or until a skewer inserted into the cake comes out clean. If the cake starts to become too brown, cover with foil or baking parchment and continue cooking. Allow to cool in the tin for 10 minutes before turning out onto a wire rack to cool completely.

MAKES 1 LARGE LOAF
PREPARATION TIME: 20 minutes
COOKING TIME: 1¼ hours

4 ripe bananas
2 eggs
1 tsp vanilla extract
125 g butter, softened
250 g plain flour, sieved
2 tsp baking powder
½ tsp salt
1 tsp mixed spice
125 g caster sugar
50 g sunflower seeds, with a
   few reserved for garnish

VIENNESE SHORTBREADS

MAKES ABOUT 20
PREPARATION TIME: 15 minutes
COOKING TIME: 10 minutes

150 g butter
5 Tbsp icing sugar
125 g plain flour, sieved
Pinch of salt
Chocolate chips, chopped
   glacé cherries or
   crystallised ginger for
   topping

Meltingly buttery, these shortbreads look professional because they are piped onto the baking tray – but they are so simple to do. Chocolate chips are our favourite topping, but glacé cherries or crystallised ginger are delicious, too.

1 Preheat the oven to 200°C/Gas Mark 6. Lightly butter two baking trays.

2 Cream the butter and sugar together until light and fluffy using the flat beater; start on a slow speed and get slightly faster. Beat in the flour and the salt, adding it in three batches, and beating well after each addition until the mixture is smooth. Continue beating until the mixture is soft enough to pipe through an icing bag.

3 Using an icing bag with a large star nozzle tip, pipe the mixture onto the baking trays in small rosette shapes. Top with chocolate chips or the topping of your choice.

4 Bake for about 10 minutes, until just set and very lightly golden. Do not allow the shortbreads to brown.

5 Cool on a wire tray.

ROCK BUNS

MAKES 12
PREPARATION TIME: 15 minutes
COOKING TIME: 25 to 30
   minutes

100 g butter, cut into small
   pieces
250 g self-raising flour
Pinch of salt
1 tsp mixed spice
100 g Demerara sugar
150 g mixed dried cake fruit,
   such as currants, raisins,
   sultanas and chopped peel
1 egg, beaten
Milk to mix

Sometimes the simplest recipes are the best! These have always been a strong favourite with both of us – and our families.

1 Preheat the oven to 200°C/Gas Mark 6. Lightly butter a 12-hole bun tin.

2 Blend the butter into the flour, salt and spice using the flat beater until the mixture resembles fine breadcrumbs. Add the sugar and fruit and mix again, then add the egg and just enough milk to make a really firm dough.

3 Scoop the mixture into the prepared tin, leaving the buns roughly shaped on top. Scatter a little extra sugar over each one and bake for 25 to 30 minutes, until golden brown and set.

4 Cool on a wire rack before serving.

TRADITIONAL SWISS ROLL

SERVES 6 TO 8
PREPARATION TIME: 40 minutes
COOKING TIME: 8 to 10 minutes

3 eggs, at room temperature
150 g caster sugar
1 tsp vanilla extract
150 g plain flour, sieved
3 to 4 Tbsp strawberry jam
Icing sugar for dusting

It is so easy to make a Swiss roll with your mixer because it does all the hard work for you. This recipe is certainly best eaten on the day it is made and can be filled with the preserve of your choice – strawberry jam is still our favourite!

1 Preheat the oven to 220°C/Gas Mark 7. Line a Swiss-roll tin with baking parchment.

2 Whisk the eggs and sugar together until the mixture is pale and thick and leaves a trail when you lift out the wire whip. This will take 10 minutes or more. Add the vanilla extract and whisk again.

3 Sieve the flour into the mixture, add the extract and fold in lightly using a metal spoon. Pour into the prepared tin and spread lightly into the corners to level out the mixture. Bake for 8 to 10 minutes or until just firm to the touch.

4 Sprinkle caster sugar over a large piece of baking parchment on a wire rack and turn the cake out onto it. Peel the baked lining paper off the cake and trim the edges with a sharp knife. Roll the cake and baking parchment up together in a tight roll and leave to cool.

5 When cool, unroll the cake and spread it with the strawberry jam, leaving a 2.5-cm gap around the edges. Roll the cake again, this time without the paper! Dust with sieved icing sugar and cut into thick slices to serve.

HONEY AND APPLE MUESLI SQUARES

These bars are so quick and easy to make and go really well with a cup of tea. The cornmeal adds some bite to the mixture and the honey and apple provide natural sweetness. These bars seem positively healthy!

....

1 Preheat the oven to 190°C/Gas Mark 5. Grease a 23-cm square baking tin.

2 Place the flours and icing sugar in the mixer bowl, add the cornmeal and the muesli and combine using the flat beater. Add the butter and blend on a medium setting until the mixture resembles breadcrumbs. Add enough cold water (probably only about 1 to 2 tablespoons) to bind the mixture together while still retaining a crumbly appearance.

3 Press two-thirds of the mixture into the prepared tin and pack it down firmly. Drizzle the honey over this base followed by the apple in an even layer. Crumble the remaining mixture over the top and press down very lightly. Bake for about 30 minutes or until golden in colour. Remove from the oven and cut immediately into bars.

4 Allow to cool completely in the tin. Store in an airtight container.

MAKES ABOUT 16 TO 20 SQUARES
PREPARATION TIME: 15 minutes
COOKING TIME: 30 minutes

200 g wholemeal flour
25 g plain flour
50 g icing sugar, sieved
50 g cornmeal or instant polenta
100 g muesli
200 g butter, chilled and diced
Cold water to mix
3 Tbsp honey
2 eating apples, peeled, cored and grated

LEMONADE SCONES

This is an amazing recipe given to us by an Australian cousin named Marlene. From the minimal list of ingredients, it's hard to imagine the perfect light and tasty end product. This quantity makes a large batch of scones but they freeze well and rarely last long anyway!

MAKES 20 TO 25 SCONES
PREPARATION TIME: 15 minutes
COOKING TIME: 10 to 15 minutes

750 g self-raising flour
375-ml can lemonade
280 ml/1¼ cups double cream
¼ tsp salt
Milk for topping (optional)

1 Preheat the oven to 200°C/Gas Mark 6. Grease and flour one or two large baking trays.

2 Sieve the flour into the mixer bowl, add the remaining ingredients and blend using the dough hook on the slowest possible setting. It is essential that this step is carried out at the slowest speed to obtain the correct consistency of dough.

3 Turn the dough out onto a lightly floured surface. The dough will be light and fluffy and will need only a gentle helping hand to pat it out to about a 2-cm thickness.

4 Cut into rounds with a 5-cm pastry cutter that's been dipped in flour, or cut into triangles with a sharp knife. Place on the baking tray, brush with a little milk if you wish and bake towards the top of the oven for 10 to 15 minutes, or until well risen and lightly golden.

5 Transfer to a wire rack to cool. Serve split and buttered, with jam and plenty of whipped cream.

COOK'S TIP: Use the lemonade at room temperature for the best results. The dough hook is the right attachment for this recipe – it's not a mistake!

DOUBLE CHOCOLATE AND ROASTED HAZELNUT BROWNIES

MAKES ABOUT 20 SQUARES
PREPARATION TIME: 20 minutes
COOKING TIME: 30 minutes

300 g luxury dark chocolate
200 g butter
200 g caster sugar
3 eggs
2 Tbsp Frangelico liqueur (for grown-ups!)
75 g self-raising flour
75 g roasted hazelnuts, chopped
100 g white chocolate chips

This sumptuous brownie recipe is wonderfully chocolaty and the addition of the roasted hazelnuts gives it a delicious crunch. Cut into small squares for a snack, or serve in larger pieces with ice cream and a drizzle of melted chocolate for dessert – or as a meal in itself!!

1 Preheat the oven to 190°C/Gas Mark 5. Grease and line the base of a 23-cm square baking tin with baking parchment.

2 Melt the chocolate with the butter (we usually use the microwave to do this; it takes about two minutes on high. The chocolate will not look melted, but stir thoroughly and you will see that this is not the case).

3 Beat the sugar and eggs thoroughly using the flat beater, then with the motor still running, gradually drizzle in the melted chocolate mixture and the Frangelico if you are using it. Allow to cool slightly and then add the flour and hazelnuts and mix to combine. Finally, add the white chocolate chips and fold in briefly on the lowest setting.

4 Pour the mixture into the prepared tin and bake for about 25 to 30 minutes or until just set. Remove from the oven and allow to cool in the tin. Cut into brownie-sized squares, or big ones if you're a real chocoholic!

APRICOT AND BUTTERMILK MUFFINS

These muffins couldn't be easier to make and are seriously tasty hot or cold – split them open and eat with a pat of butter or add some whipped cream! You can adapt the recipe by swapping the apricots for another dried fruit (dried cranberries are a real success) or by adding spices such as ginger or cinnamon.

1 Preheat the oven to 200°C/Gas Mark 6. Line a 12-hole muffin tin with paper liners.

2 Combine the dry ingredients and mix thoroughly. Set aside.

3 Combine the remaining ingredients using the flat beater. Pour the dry ingredients into the mixer bowl and blend on the slowest speed setting. Do not beat the mixture; just fold together and do not worry about leaving lumps.

4 Using a small ladle, fill each muffin case about three-quarters full. Bake for about 20 to 25 minutes until firm and golden. Serve hot or cold.

COOK'S TIP: You can chop the apricots using the coarse shredding drum of the Rotary Slicer and Shredder. If you are unable to buy buttermilk, simply sour fresh milk with 1 teaspoon lemon juice and allow to stand for 15 minutes at room temperature before using.

MAKES ABOUT 12 LARGE MUFFINS
PREPARATION TIME: 15 minutes
COOKING TIME: 25 to 30 minutes

250 g plain flour, sieved
1 Tbsp baking powder
½ tsp salt
75 g sugar
1 Tbsp grated orange zest
100 g dried apricots, finely chopped
250 ml/1 cup buttermilk
80 ml/⅓ cup melted butter
1 egg, beaten

STICKY DATE AND COCONUT SLICES

MAKES ABOUT 8 TO 10 SLICES
PREPARATION TIME: 10 minutes
COOKING TIME: 30 minutes

100 g butter
1 Tbsp golden syrup
1 egg, beaten
150 g chopped dates
150 g Demerara sugar
100 g desiccated coconut
125 g self-raising flour

This recipe is from a restaurant in New Zealand, which offers an amazing array of slices, bars and pancakes. These are a particular favourite and are wonderfully sweet and sticky to eat!

1 Preheat the oven to 160°C/Gas Mark 3. Grease an 18-cm square baking tin.

2 Melt the butter and syrup together in a saucepan and then allow to cool slightly, for about five minutes.

3 In the mixer bowl combine all the dry ingredients, then add the melted mixture and the egg and mix thoroughly using the flat beater. Pour the mixture into the tin and press down evenly.

4 Bake for about 30 minutes or until well risen and golden. The cake will be slightly soft in the centre, but will become firm when cool. Cool in the tin before cutting into slices

COFFEE CRUNCH COOKIES

These cookies are really light and crisp – they often spread into strange shapes in the oven, but maybe that is part of their attraction.

1 Preheat the oven to 200°C/Gas Mark 6. Lightly grease two baking trays. Sieve together the flour and baking powder.

2 Heat the butter slowly until melted, then simmer it for five minutes. Combine the sugar and coffee in the mixer bowl, add the hot butter, mix briefly with the flat beater and then leave to cool for five minutes.

3 Add the egg and beat until thick and creamy, then gradually work in the flour to make a soft and shiny yet manageable dough.

4 Roll the mixture into walnut-sized pieces in your hands, place on the prepared baking trays and flatten lightly with a fork. Allow plenty of room for the cookies to spread, but if they join up in the oven you can break them apart later.

5 Bake for 12 to15 minutes, until golden brown. Allow to cool slightly on the trays before transferring to a wire rack to cool completely and to become crisp.

COOK'S TIP: Once the cookies are completely cold, store in an airtight container.

MAKES ABOUT 30 COOKIES
PREPARATION TIME: 20 minutes
COOKING TIME: 12 to 15 minutes

325 g plain flour
2 tsp baking powder
200 g unsalted butter
200 g caster sugar
2 Tbsp freeze-dried instant coffee granules
1 egg, beaten
Caster sugar for dredging (optional)

BREADS AND BUNS

Home-made bread offers so much more in the way of flavour and texture than store bought bread, especially when purchased from supermarkets and convenience stores. We both prefer to use fresh yeast but it is not always available, so for convenience, we have created all these recipes for easy blend dry yeast. A big advantage to this is that these doughs require just one rising period, making the whole preparation and baking time much shorter.

TOMATO AND OLIVE OIL BREAD

MAKES 1 LARGE LOAF
PREPARATION TIME: 3 hours,
  including rising
COOKING TIME: 25 to 30
  minutes

500 g strong plain flour
1 Tbsp salt
7 g sachet easy blend
  dry yeast
100 ml/½ cup olive oil
300 ml/1½ cups lukewarm
  water
12 cherry tomatoes, halved
1 to 2 cloves garlic, very finely
  sliced
Olive oil and coarse sea salt
  for topping

Much faster to prepare than a traditional focaccia, this olive oil bread is enlivened with sweet cherry tomatoes and a little fresh garlic. It's delicious served with soft fresh goat's cheese and a salad.

1 Blend the flour, salt and yeast together on a low speed using the dough hook, then add the olive oil and most of the water. Mix, and knead thoroughly on a low speed, adding enough water to make a soft but manageable dough. The kneading will take about five to six minutes.

2 Scrape the dough off the hook back into the bowl. Cover with clingfilm and leave in a warm place for two hours until well risen.

3 Return the bowl to the mixer and knead the dough again to its original size with the dough hook on speed 2. Turn out onto a lightly floured surface.

4 Generously oil a small rectangular roasting tin (about 20 x 25 cm). Divide the dough in half and roll out one piece to roughly fit the base of the tin, stretching it into the corners. Cover with the halved tomatoes and garlic and season lightly with salt and pepper. Roll out the remaining dough and place it over the tomatoes. Cover the pan with clingfilm and leave in a warm place again for about 20 minutes, until just starting to rise.

5 Preheat the oven to 220°C/Gas Mark 7. Carefully make indentations all over the dough with your fingertips; this will seal the two halves together and stop the dough from rising too much. Drizzle with a little olive oil and sprinkle with coarse sea salt, then bake for 25 to 30 minutes, until golden brown.

6 Cool on a wire rack before serving.

RUSTIC OLIVE BREAD

Here is a country-style bread, heavy with the oil and fruits of the olive. The richness of the dough means that it is slow to rise, but the flavour is fabulous. Ensure that the olives are well drained before adding them to the dough, or the bread will become heavy and difficult to handle. Use stuffed olives if you like – those with jalapeno peppers are especially good.

MAKES 1 LARGE LOAF
PREPARATION TIME: 2 hours,
    including rising
COOKING TIME: 30 minutes

500 g strong plan flour
1 tsp salt
7 g sachet easy blend dry
    yeast
100 ml/½ cup good-quality
    extra-virgin olive oil
About 300 ml/1½ cups
    lukewarm water
150 g stoned green olives,
    roughly chopped

1 Blend the flour, salt and yeast together in the mixer bowl with the dough hook, then add the oil and most of the water. Mix to a manageable dough, adding more water if necessary, and knead thoroughly for at least five minutes.

2 Add the olives to the dough and work them in gently on a very slow speed.

3 Turn the dough out onto a lightly floured surface, shape into a round loaf and then place on an oiled baking tray. Cover and leave in a warm place to rise for one to one and a half hours, until doubled in size.

4 Preheat the oven to 220°C/Gas Mark 7. Brush the loaf with a little extra olive oil if you wish. Bake for 30 minutes, until the base sounds hollow when tapped and the loaf is lightly golden. Cool on a wire rack and break into rough chunks to serve.

LIGHT RYE BREAD

This is a basic bread recipe that can be used for almost any flour – vary the quantities of white and wholemeal or rye flour as you wish. Use the same method for an all-white bread, too. For this rye loaf, we have used half rye and half white flour, giving a moist crumb with a crispy crust.

MAKES I LOAF

PREPARATION TIME: 1½ hours,
  including rising

COOKING TIME: 35 to 40
  minutes

250 g strong plain flour
250 g rye flour
2 tsp salt
7 g sachet easy blend
  dry yeast
3 Tbsp olive oil
400 ml/2 cups warm water

1 Mix the flours, salt and yeast in the mixer bowl, then add the oil and most of the water. Mix to a manageable dough using the dough hook, adding a little more water if necessary. Knead thoroughly for five to six minutes until smooth.

2 Shape the dough on a lightly floured surface into a round loaf and place on an oiled baking tray. Cover and leave in a warm place to rise for about one hour, until doubled in size.

3 Preheat the oven to 220°C/Gas Mark 7. Scatter a little more flour (rye or white) over the loaf and bake for 35 to 40 minutes. The crust should be well browned and the base of the loaf will sound hollow when tapped. Cool on a wire rack.

BARA BRITH

This richly fruited sweet loaf is a traditional recipe from Wales and is often served sliced and buttered for an afternoon snack. It is slow to rise because it contains a great deal of fruit, which is worked into the dough after the main kneading to preserve the colour of the bread's crumb. This can be a real effort to make by hand and is much easier with the mixer.

MAKES I LARGE LOAF
PREPARATION TIME: 2 to 2 ½
 hours, including rising
COOKING TIME: 35 to 40
 minutes

50 g butter
375 g strong white flour
I tsp salt
2 Tbsp caster sugar
½ tsp mixed spice
7 g sachet easy blend
 dry yeast
I egg, beaten
150 ml/⅔ cup lukewarm water
300 g mixed dried fruit, such
 as currants, raisins, sultanas
 and chopped peel
Milk or beaten egg and
 caster sugar for topping

I Rub the butter into the flour and salt using the flat beater, then add the sugar, spice and yeast and blend again.

2 Add the egg and water and mix to a soft but not sticky dough using the dough hook. Knead for about five minutes until smooth, adding a little more water if necessary.

3 Gradually knead in the fruit using the dough hook; it may be necessary to turn the dough over in the fruit in the bowl once or twice by hand during this process as the fruit may collect under the dough.

4 Turn out onto a lightly floured surface and gently shape into a smooth round; try to make sure that all the fruit on the top is coated in dough, even just very thinly, as this will stop the fruit from burning in the oven. Place the loaf on a greased baking tray, cover and leave in a warm place for two hours or even longer, until well risen.

5 Preheat the oven to 180°C/Gas Mark 4. Brush the loaf with milk or a little beaten egg, dredge lightly with sugar and then bake for 35 to 40 minutes, until golden brown. (The Bara Brith is a bit too rich really to sound hollow when tapped on the base, so don't use it as a test for doneness.)

6 Cool on a wire rack. Serve sliced and buttered.

STOLLEN

MAKES 2 LOAVES

PREPARATION TIME: about 2 hours, including rising

COOKING TIME: 30 minutes

7 g sachet easy blend dry yeast

1 tsp caster sugar

500 g plain flour

150 ml/⅔ cup lukewarm milk

Pinch of salt

3 Tbsp light brown sugar, or light Muscovado sugar if available

50 g butter, cut into slices, plus a little extra for finishing

2 eggs, beaten

1 Tbsp rum

150 g mixed dried fruit, such as currants, raisins, sultanas and chopped peel

Grated rind of half a lemon

150 g prepared marzipan or almond paste

Icing sugar for dredging

These traditional Christmas loaves are found all over northern Europe, although they originally hail from Germany. The secret of a successful marzipan-filled stollen is not to place the marzipan right on the fold of the bread, or it may well spring open during rising or baking. Tie with a ribbon to make a tasty gift for friends. Plain flour is used so that the stollen are not too light and doughy.

....

1 Blend the yeast, caster sugar, 125 g of flour and the milk together in the mixer bowl. Cover and leave in a warm place for at least an hour, until it starts to become frothy.

2 Add the remaining flour, salt, brown sugar, butter, most (not all!) of the beaten eggs and the rum and mix to a manageable dough with the dough hook, adding a little extra milk if necessary. Knead thoroughly for five minutes, then cover and leave in a warm place for an hour, or until doubled in size.

3 Knead the dough lightly, then gently work in the dried fruit and lemon rind using the dough hook. Do not over-knead. Turn out onto a lightly floured surface and divide into two. Shape into ovals, about 1.5 cm thick..

4 Roll the marzipan into two even lengths to fit the length of the stollen. Press the rolling pin into the dough to make an indentation about one-third of the way from the bottom of each oval. Lay the marzipan in the marked places then fold the dough over towards you, leaving the ends of the marzipan just showing if possible. Seal the edges with some of the remaining beaten egg. Place the stollens on a lightly buttered baking tray, cover and leave to rise again for about 30 minutes.

5 Preheat the oven to 180°C/Gas Mark 4. Brush the dough with any remaining egg and bake for 30 minutes, or until golden brown.

6 Cool on a wire rack. Melt a little extra butter and brush over the cooled stollens and then top with sieved icing sugar.

SPANISH-STYLE SEEDED LOAF

This olive oil bread is heavy with toasted nuts and seeds – it's fabulous with soup, cheeses or spicy meats like chorizo sausage. We usually don't add the extras until we have kneaded the dough, but in this case, it is actually a good thing to really knead them into the dough because it allows the nuts and seeds to break up a little.

....

1 Toast the hazelnuts and pine kernels until golden brown, either in a dry frying pan or under the grill. Cool slightly, then place in the mixer bowl with the remaining dry ingredients. Add the oil and most of the water, then mix to a pliable, manageable dough using the dough hook. Add extra water if necessary, but feel the dough first.

2 Knead thoroughly for about six minutes on a slow speed.

3 Turn out onto a floured surface and lightly knead the dough by hand until smooth, then shape into a round loaf. Place on an oiled baking tray and leave to rise in a warm place for about one hour, until doubled in size.

4 Preheat the oven to 220°C/Gas Mark 7. Dust the loaf lightly with flour and then bake for 30 to 35 minutes, or until the base sounds hollow when tapped. Cool before eating.

MAKES 1 LARGE LOAF
PREPARATION TIME: 1 hour 15 minutes, including rising
COOKING TIME: 30 to 35 minutes

50 g hazelnuts, roughly chopped
2 Tbsp pine kernels
500 g strong plain flour
1 tsp salt
50 g pumpkin seeds, or pumpkin and sunflower seeds mixed
2 Tbsp sesame seeds
7 g sachet easy blend dry yeast
5 Tbsp extra-virgin olive oil
250 to 280 ml/1 to 1¼ cups lukewarm water

APPLE AND CINNAMON DOUGHNUTS

MAKES 8

PREPARATION TIME : 1 ¼ hours

COOKING TIME : about 10 minutes

250 g plain flour

½ tsp salt

2 tsp easy blend dry yeast

1 Tbsp sunflower or vegetable oil

1 egg, beaten

150 ml/⅔ cup warm water

1 eating apple, peeled and cut into 6-mm dice

Oil for deep-frying

Caster sugar and ground cinnamon for coating

Home-made doughnuts just have to be one of the most fun and special things we make! These days, you can get jam in a squirt bottle, which could be used to fill the doughnuts, but we salve our consciences by making apple doughnuts, thinking that the fruit will be good for us!

1 Mix the flour, salt and yeast together in the mixer bowl, then add the oil, egg and most of the water. Mix to a manageable dough with the dough hook, adding a little more water if necessary, then knead thoroughly for five to six minutes until smooth and elastic. Cover the bowl and leave in a warm place to rise for about one hour, until doubled in size.

2 Cut eight small squares of baking parchment and bring a large pan of water to the boil. Knead the dough again lightly with the dough hook, then turn out onto a lightly floured surface and divide into eight pieces. Knead each piece until smooth and form into discs. Place a little of the apple on each one and shape the dough around it, pinching the edges together to seal. Place each doughnut on a piece of baking parchment, sealed side down, and leave for 10 minutes.

3 Heat the oil for frying until it reaches 180°C on a thermometer inserted in the oil. Lift the doughnuts with the paper, to avoid causing the risen dough to fall back. Blanch the doughnuts in the boiling water for just a few seconds; the paper will float off and you can skim it out of the pan. Remove the doughnuts with a slotted spoon and drain on crumpled kitchen paper.

4 Fry the doughnuts in the oil for six to eight minutes, turning once, until golden brown. They will "grow" during cooking, so cook no more than four at a time. Drain on kitchen paper and then toss in the sugar and cinnamon. Allow to cool before eating.

COURGETTE ROLLS

This recipe yields a moist white bread, which is perfect with soups, cheeses and cold meats. Grate the courgettes with the Rotary Slicer and Shredder and squeeze as much moisture out as possible before salting. This is a necessary process and not just a whim; otherwise, the dough becomes too wet during kneading and is very difficult to handle.

....

1 Grate the courgettes coarsely using the Rotary Slicer and Shredder; catch it in a clean tea towel placed over the mixer bowl and then, wrapping the courgettes in the cloth, squeeze out as much water as possible. Place the courgettes in a colander, sprinkle generously with salt and leave for one hour. Rinse thoroughly with cold water and then squeeze dry again in your hands.

2 Mix the courgettes with the flour, measured salt and yeast in the mixer bowl, then add the oil and most of the water. Mix to a dough with the dough hook; the dough should be a bit drier than usual to allow for any extra juices coming out of the courgettes during kneading. Knead for five to six minutes, adding a little extra water if necessary.

3 Divide the dough into eight pieces and shape into rolls, placing them in an oiled 25-cm round springform tin. Cover and leave in a warm place to rise for about an hour.

4 Preheat the oven to 220°C/Gas Mark 7. Brush the top of the rolls with a little beaten egg – decadent yes, but it gives a soft yet wonderfully golden crust – and bake for 30 minutes. Remove from the pan, cool and tear apart to eat.

MAKES 8
PREPARATION TIME: 2½ hours,
  including salting and rising
COOKING TIME: 30 minutes

150 g courgettes, trimmed
  (about 2 medium
  courgettes)
Salt (see method)
375 g strong plain flour
I tsp salt
7 g sachet easy blend dry
  yeast
I Tbsp sunflower or vegetable
  oil
About 200 ml/I cup warm
  water
Beaten egg for glazing

MORNING ROLLS

MAKES 12

PREPARATION TIME: overnight rising, plus 45 minutes

COOKING TIME: 20 to 25 minutes

FOR THE OVERNIGHT DOUGH:

375 g strong plain flour

2 tsp salt

7 g sachet easy blend dry yeast, divided (use 1 tsp and save the rest)

500 ml/2 cups cold water

FOR THE MORNING DOUGH:

100 ml/½ cup warm water

500 g strong plain flour

50 g butter, cut into small pieces

1 tsp caster sugar

Start the first dough just as you go to bed, then get up early the next day to finish the mixing and to shape the rolls. It really is worth the effort, especially when you have guests staying overnight. The long rising time gives the rolls a soft, creamy texture and a real depth of flavour.

....

1 Make the overnight dough, starting just before bed the night before you want to serve them. Place the flour, salt and 1 teaspoon yeast in the bowl, add the water and just combine to make a lumpy dough. Cover the bowl with clingfilm and leave in the kitchen until morning.

2 The next day, make the morning dough. To the same bowl with the overnight dough, add the water, flour, butter, sugar and the remaining yeast. Mix thoroughly using the dough hook and then knead for about six minutes, until the dough is smooth and elastic.

3 On a lightly floured surface, shape the dough into 12 rolls and place on an oiled Swiss-roll tin. Cover and leave for 30 minutes in a warm place.

4 Preheat the oven to 200°C/Gas Mark 6. Bake the rolls for 20 to 25 minutes, until lightly golden. The rolls should look cooked on the base; they will not be crusty enough really to sound hollow when tapped.

CHELSEA BUNS

Although we have used easy blend dry yeast for these delicious fruited buns, we have still given the dough two full rising periods, plus an extra fermentation for the yeast at the beginning. This ensures a really light result with a good creamy texture and flavour. We like icing on our buns, so we've included that too!

1 Place 75 g flour in a bowl with the yeast and milk, cover and leave in a warm place for 30 minutes or until it begins slowly to ferment.

2 Mix the salt with the remaining flour in the mixer bowl, add half the butter and blend it in using the flat beater. Add the yeast mixture and the egg and mix to a soft dough using the dough hook; add a little more milk or water if necessary. Knead thoroughly to make a soft, ever so slightly sticky dough that leaves the sides of the bowl easily during kneading. Continue to knead for five minutes on a low to medium speed.

3 Cover the bowl and leave in a warm place for about an hour and a half, until the dough is well risen and has doubled in size. Knead gently again using the dough hook. Melt the remaining butter and allow it to cool.

4 Roll the dough out on a lightly floured surface to a rectangle about 30 x 20 cm. Turn the dough around after each rolling and pull out the corners with your fingers to keep the rectangular shape.

5 Brush the dough generously with most of the melted butter, then use the remainder to grease a 25-cm round springform tin. Mix the fruit with the brown sugar and sprinkle it evenly over the dough before rolling up from one of the long sides. Cut the dough into eight slices and arrange them in the prepared tin.

6 Cover the tin again and leave for another 30 minutes, until the buns have risen and are puffy and start to spread towards each other.

7 Preheat the oven to 190°C/Gas Mark 5 and bake the buns for 30 to 35 minutes. Allow to cool slightly in the tin.

8 Blend the icing sugar with a little water, then drizzle it over the warm buns. Leave to set before removing the buns from the tin, breaking them apart. Serve buttered if you are feeling very decadent!

MAKES 8
PREPARATION TIME: 2½ to 3 hours, including rising
COOKING TIME: 30 to 35 minutes

250 g strong plain flour
7 g sachet easy blend dry yeast
100 ml/½ cup lukewarm milk
½ tsp salt
50 g butter
1 egg, beaten
100 g mixed dried fruit, such as currants, raisins, sultanas and chopped peel
50 g light brown sugar, or light Muscovado sugar if available
75 g icing sugar, sieved

INDEX

ACKNOWLEDGEMENTS

Mixers have been a part of my life for as long as I have been making a living, in one way or another, with food. So many thanks to the TDA Test Kitchen, and especially to Val Collins, my first boss. Also to Linda Kirk and all the Kenwood team, at home and all around the world, who taught me so much.

A big Thank You to Claire Small, who tested some of the recipes on work experience from school and was the most enormous help. Your constructive comments were greatly appreciated and good luck in finding a cooking career - you'll be fabulous!

Special thanks to my husband Nick who has eaten every single one of my recipes in this and countless other books, and remains just one trouser size larger than when we married 21 years ago! And to all my friends and colleagues who bake and keep the art of home cooking alive.

ROSEMARY MOON

My thanks go to the marvellous Mrs Moon for making this, and so much else, possible; and to Anna and Peta for setting me off in the first place! A big mention to my Ozzie support team who have inspired me throughout the planning and writing of this book – your friendship, kindness, and ability to be completely silly, will never be forgotten – Scotty and Dominico in Dubbo; the Team at Café Café, Subiaco; Dennis and Scarlet in Noggerup. Most importantly to my Australian family – The Foodies Extraordinaire at Starlings; and champion cake maker Mummy Marlene.

To my darling Daddy and my wonderful brother Si, who between them, bravely ate their way through each recipe test without complaint, and to my Mum who encouraged me to bake my first cake and has encouraged me ever since.

KATIE BISHOP

The Publisher would like to thank the team at Wild Card Public Relations, especially Jen Eveleigh, for help with the loan of KitchenAid mixers.

KitchenAid mixers can be bought across the world.
Visit the website at www.kitchenAid.com.

Customer service centers:

USA:
P.O. Box 218
St. Joseph
MI 49085
1-800-541-6390

Europe:
KitchenAid Europa
Nijverheidslaan
3-Box 5
B-1853
Strombeek-Bever
Belgium

UK:
CAD
Apuro Ltd
Unit 21A
Monkspath Business Park
Solihull, B90 4NZ
0845 450 0099

Australia:
55 Broadmeadow Road
Broadmeadow NSW 2298
Help Desk phone line: 1800 990 990

When using the grinder and sausage stuffer to make sausages, natural casings are required. These can be mail-ordered from:

International Casings Group
4420 S. Woolcott,
Chicago,
IL 60609, USA
www.casings.com

or

Spicetech UK,
Whaley Bridge,
Derbyshire SK23 7AZ
www.spicetech.co.uk